get your life back on track

NOW

IEVA ELZA ZAHAROVA

Ieva Elza Zaharova
get your life back on track NOW

Cover graphic design Ieva Zaharova
Layout formatting Ieva Zaharova

Publisher Ieva Zaharova, 2023

ISBN 978-9934-23-975-5

For all who want to create
the best life for themselves.

TABLE OF CONTENTS

We all have dreams we want to fulfill, goals to achieve, and manifestations we eagerly await. Yet, for some reason, they have not materialized. There's a constant feeling of being held back, and at times, the temptation to give up lingers, accepting the notion that 'this is life.' But then, why do other people in the world can get anything they want? Why do some people achieve their goals?

The concept of 'manifestation' has gained increasing attention. What does it truly mean? To manifest your desires, dreams, and goals, mere visualization is not sufficient. Photos on your phone, posters on the wall, entries in a diary—while they may help, the question persists: Why hasn't it all come to fruition? Manifestation, in essence, is 'the practice of bringing something into your life through faith.' However, faith involves 'accepting that something exists or is true.' In simpler terms, it all boils down to your mindset.

Manifestation only works when you believe you already

possess it, when your body senses it as a reality. This is your truth. Merely thinking about your dream job, house, appearance, or any other goal won't cut it. You must KNOW. You have to embrace your truth and regard it as a reality because, at any moment, everything can manifest into existence.

However, the challenge lies in the fact that we don't always have complete control over our thoughts. Countless limiting beliefs are deeply embedded in our subconscious, often operating beneath our conscious awareness. This book delves into the crucial aspect of tuning in to your subconscious, eliminating these limiting thoughts, and forging a new identity. Central to this transformation is the concept of neuroplasticity— the ability of the brain to undergo structural and functional changes.

This relatively recent scientific development has demonstrated that our brain's activity can be altered. So, if your current thought patterns haven't propelled you toward your desired goals, it becomes evident that a shift in thinking is necessary. By discarding outdated and unproductive thought patterns, you pave the way to establish a new identity aligned with your aspirations. This process enables you to live authentically and attract everything you desire or, perhaps, even something better.

The initial and fundamental task is to cultivate a genuine love for our lives, embracing gratitude for the present moment. I believe in the immense value of this practice. When we take things for granted, we inadvertently diminish their significance. However, by appreciating every person, every event, and, most importantly, ourselves and our positive qualities, we cultivate a sense of perfection that enables us to attract similar positivity.

Taking something for granted turns it into something dispensable. On the contrary, by valuing every aspect of our lives, we create a foundation for continued attraction of similar positive experiences. As the saying goes, 'you are what you think about.' Once we develop love and appreciation for our current state, feel secure, and realize our dreams, we can then shift our energy to align with our goals or embark on the journey of manifestation.

Persisting thoughts about the past divert our energy, hindering our ability to act as magnets for all the good things life has to offer. It's crucial to choose to change our thinking, aligning it with the energy of our desired manifestations. Destructive thoughts generate corresponding emotions in the body, disrupting our ability to attract positivity.

The beauty lies in the fact that everything is changeable! My goal is not to guide you on a one-time lottery win, but to help you consistently attract and embody your true self. This book is not about chance; it's about conscious self-transformation—shedding old traumas and enhancing yourself. The ultimate aim is for you to confidently declare, 'I am beautiful, healthy, rich, smart, helpful, brave'—whatever you genuinely desire for yourself.

The freedom of the mind is just four steps away, achieved through the development of four essential qualities. The speed at which results manifest depends on the volume of your truth and the depth of your self-belief. Additionally, it hinges on how adeptly you navigate and overcome any obstacles that attempt to pull you back into the old reality. Undoubtedly, there will be 'tests,' but the key is to learn not to assign undue significance to them, but rather to view them as a natural part of the transformative process.

Changing your identity involves gaining awareness of your desires, reassessing your choices, and making necessary adjustments by discarding old habits and embracing new ones. It requires courage, a broadened perception, the cultivation of patience, and other aspects that we will explore further in this book. However, your primary objective is to shift your thinking.

I believe that within this book, you will discover insights previously unexplored in relation to your life. Perhaps it will be enough to initiate a 'click' or, in scientific terms, form a new neural connection, prompting you to think new, improved thoughts about yourself and, consequently, enhancing the world around you.

Cherish your life! Embrace yourself! Recognize your freedom and the potential to attain everything you desire! Take charge of your mind! You were created to fulfill yourself, and I extend my heartfelt wishes for your success.

May your new life be beautiful!

WHAT IS FREEDOM

How often do you conceive an idea that you want to bring to life, only to encounter a swift "but..."? Can you confidently declare that every action, every pursuit is driven by a genuine desire? Are you the architect of your own life? If you find yourself holding this book, chances are you may not be entirely content with your response to one of the aforementioned questions. By continuing to read, you acknowledge that you've already taken a significant step toward generating positive responses and, simultaneously, constructing your optimal life. That's no small feat.

We might contemplate - "I'm fine just the way I am, and there's no need for change." And indeed, that's true! Each person is inherently remarkable as they are. So why write a book about crafting the best version of yourself and, consequently, embracing change? Why do more and more individuals feel disoriented in the course of their lives, suddenly grappling with an identity crisis, only to realize over time that they yearn for something else? There's a prevailing belief that individuals cannot change, let alone change others. There's some truth in that notion. However, every situation can be examined from various perspectives.

I contend that we have ALREADY undergone change. We are ALREADY transformed. It hasn't always been a matter of our free choice. People, events, our surroundings, habits... There are numerous aspects that elude our daily attention. Consequently, we fail to recognize how profoundly they impact us. And significantly so! We don't always grasp, recall, or willingly acknowledge the extent to which our surroundings influence us. Yet, when we do realize it, we inexplicably assign significance to these events and permit them to shape our future lives. But if everyone permits monumental global events to reshape us, won't we all become too... similar? So, who are we, individually?

Throughout our lives, we encounter an immeasurable number of people—each with a distinct purpose, each offering a lesson, leaving behind memories, imparting knowledge. As we navigate life, we often find ourselves gradually drifting away from our true nature, from our authentic selves. This journey begins from the moment we are born. Growing up under the influence of parents, teachers, and society, we may not always assert our desires and opinions. The longing to express our truth is frequently stifled or even condemned. Consequently, we become a compilation of others' influences, leading to potential conflicts with our true selves as the years pass.

As we mature, we encounter contradictions and challenges in pursuing our dreams. The life we've been taught may not align with our vision of happiness or may not allow us to discern the purpose of our existence. Therefore, when asserting that a person cannot change, we must bear in mind that change has already occurred. This book serves as a guide, not only to rediscover your original, authentic self but also to understand how to develop in a way that fosters harmony and confidence in becoming the person you truly desire to be.

In essence, this book aims to assist you in reclaiming your authenticity and living in alignment with your identity. What is identity? We'll delve into that shortly. For now, contemplate what the best version of yourself means to YOU. How do you envision your life today, tomorrow, 30 years from now? What impression do you want to leave on others, and most importantly, what legacy do you wish to be remembered for on your hundredth birthday?

The fundamental premise for humans is continuous evolution. We engage in self-development, explore nature, and our insatiable curiosity and intuition lead us to constant discoveries. Without this drive, we might still be sitting by the fire, hunting animals, and taking occasional naps, limited to no more than three hours to prevent the fire from extinguishing or wild beasts from attacking. Interestingly, this unconscious habit of a three-hour sleep cycle is a result of our ancient ancestors. If we maintain a healthy sleep routine, we often transition into "deep sleep" shortly after falling asleep, typically awakening around the three-hour mark due to this ingrained rhythm.

Our ancestors did not have the luxury of enjoying the recommended 7-8 hours of sleep that we have today. Their primary concerns were keeping the fire alive and fending off potential attacks from coyotes or bears. It's not surprising that their life expectancy was significantly shorter, given the challenging conditions and stress of that era. While we also face stress in modern times, this book is not intended for comparison. Thanks to the perseverance of our ancestors in developing and improving living conditions, we can now relish in the privilege of a full 7-8 hours of sleep at night. Or at least, that's how it should be.

We find ourselves in an era where we have the privilege to choose where and how we want to live. Some opt for apartments, others for houses, and preferences span from apple orchards to homes with pools, forest cabins with fireplaces, the latest technology, constant travel, farms with animals, or a combination of it all. It seems idyllic, doesn't it? However, there's always a sense that something is missing or not quite as we desire. Yet, this is entirely human. The constant desire for development is normal, as is the perpetual yearning to feel better, freer, and happier. So, where does the challenge arise?

The moment we aspire to develop is when, subconsciously, we acknowledge that there might be something more—a readiness for the 'next level.' We are prepared to expand because we've already reached the "previous level." How does this process of moving to the next level work? After living the same life for an extended period, it's easy to feel like nothing is happening. This could be the point where, at the current level, you've already given what once fulfilled you. If life starts feeling repetitive, you no longer derive joy from this giving. When we're accustomed to it, we often label it as "that's life."

Consider a work situation: After a decade in the same workplace, discussions primarily revolve around colleagues, management, and unsatisfactory working conditions. Yet, can you recall the joy when you first learned about the job offer? There was a time when it was your dream, and it became a reality! At that point, you gave with joy and received with joy. Life is about a continuous give and take. When this exchange becomes devoid of value, it's likely that you've given what this place needed, unless there's shared, upward development. Everything must be in constant motion, either upward or in the opposite direction. When the ascent halts, the yearning for something new emerges because, subconsciously, we sense it's time for a new level.

This desire for change can manifest swiftly, leading us to suppress our inner voice with excuses like "I can't move because..." or "I don't deserve it because..." or "I won't be able to because..." We resist our inner voice with self-created excuses, clinging to our current work until exhaustion, perhaps seeking recognition from management or fearing the stigma of 'not lasting long enough.'

Certainly, reaching the next level is not an act of "escape." If we find ourselves stuck in a cycle of repeating the same situations, it's likely that something has gone unnoticed and remains unresolved. To ascend to the next level means embracing gratitude for what we currently have, in this very moment— the realization of our past desires. Once we've received it, expressing gratitude for everything in our lives becomes imperative every morning and every night.

However, when a new opportunity presents itself, our task is to recognize it, heed our intuition, resist limiting thoughts, and grant ourselves permission to embark on the journey of development.

YOU ALREADY HAVE EVERYTHING

Recognizing that you are currently engaged with this book emboldens me to assert that you ALREADY possess EVERYTHING. The mere fact that you somehow discovered this book, found your way to it, and are presently reading it are reasons enough to express gratitude. And yet, the lingering thoughts persist: "I would like something more...", "I crave freedom...", "but I can't because...".

Imagine for a moment: What if you could purchase freedom for just 1 cent at the supermarket right now? Would you eagerly pursue it for yourself or perhaps gift it to someone else? Whom would you choose as the recipient? Does everyone truly deserve freedom, and do they comprehend how to embrace it? How do you visualize this "product"? Is there a fear of loss?

However, I must disappoint you if you believe that freedom can be bought with money. Similarly, if you perceive money itself as freedom, or if you think someone else can bestow it upon you, I must gently unsettle those notions. The path to happiness is, in fact, straightforward: a person must be fulfilled. To be fulfilled means to be whole—a singular entity. We achieve wholeness when we exist in perfect harmony with our true nature. It boils down to strengthening your identity. It's that simple! Allow me to elaborate a bit more delicately:

* If you harbor a dream or pursue a calling, you have a goal.

* If you are certain WHY you wish to attain this goal, you hold values.

* However, if you comprehend HOW to achieve this

goal, you possess a robust identity.

While people may share similar goals and values, the varied approaches to achieving them highlight the uniqueness of each individual. This diversity underscores the notion that teaching another person might not be effective, as their identity and, consequently, their chosen path differ from yours. The key lies in remaining true to our inner convictions, paving the way for a life filled with daily fulfillment.

Living in harmony with your identity propels you toward your loftiest aspirations and dreams, creating an environment where everything seems to align in your favor. In this state, personal growth becomes a natural progression, and the need for stringent control diminishes, as you trust that the outcome will favor you regardless. Discovering your ideal "flow" allows you to let things unfold, confident that this delightful path will undoubtedly lead you to your destination. Isn't that remarkable?

Irrespective of your current life circumstances, experiences, worries, or sorrows, acknowledge that every day, you are already doing your best. Even if your daily life doesn't entirely satisfy you, as you embark on the journey back to the best version of yourself, express gratitude with the words, "Today I did the best I could." These words served as my anchor during a prolonged period of depression when getting out of bed seemed like a monumental task on certain days. Recognizing that it was the best I could do on those days was significant. It allowed me to understand in silence that "this is not who you are!" and "I'm tired of not being in my own skin!" This realization initiated a profound self-discoveryjourney to understand what was truly happening within me.

By sharing this, I want to convey that it's understandable to feel anger, guilt, and shame about oneself, especially when attempting self-improvement for an extended period. However, I am grateful for enduring this lengthy road, as it led me back to my authentic self.

WHAT DOES "CHANGE" MEAN?

Which sounds better: "Start changing!" or "Start acting on your identity!"? Which incentive calls you more to active action? Their meaning in this case is the same. If you don't live according to your calling, then you haven't created your identity yet, so you don't know who you are, so you have to change!

The structure and function of the brain are still not 100% understood, but what is currently known is that it is possible to change its activity, and this is the main thing we need to know. The brain, like other parts of the body, such as muscles, can be perfected, improved, as long as you work on it. Just as we use exercise to develop our physical form, we should also exercise our brain. Only in this way is it possible to improve them or at least maintain their health. The brain does not age - it changes, and how we will be in old age depends on how we act and, above all, think today. There are billions of neurons in the brain, and hundreds of new ones are produced every day, which means that processes are constantly taking place in the brain, and if you use them correctly, you can relatively easily change not only your thinking but also your behavior and life in general. Then, if we engage in physical activities such as running, cycling, swimming, and also sex, the number of neurons produced every day increases. It happens when the heart beats faster for at least 20 minutes. It promotes blood flow to the brain and thus the production of various growth hormones. If we do not properly "employ" these new neurons, then they join everything old - bad habits, become dull with addictions, grow with negative thoughts, and, in general, brain activity slows down because it is not developed. However, if we are physically active every day and also train the brain, for example, study, read, then it could be said that it is hardened. When we put completely new information into them, we stress them so that they know what to do and do not "rot" along with old thoughts and habits. By creating new thought forms, we can reprogram existing ones. So, if we don't degenerate our brains, then needless to say, we can't change ourselves, or it's very difficult and without long-term results. By employing the existing neurons, with which we are not completely satisfied, they will work less and less lazily, the blood in the brain will circulate more and more slowly, and in the end, we will only be left with habits formed over time. We will perform them so automatically that we will no longer be aware of what and why we are doing it and how to regulate it. Long-term results will come when you train the new neurons to work long enough for them to "overcome" the old ones and replace the old habits with ones that align with your best life.

Until the age of about 10, it is very easy for us to perceive new information, especially languages - at this time, learning them is the easiest. However, the most important stage of brain development is during adolescence. During this time, the limbic part of the brain, which is responsible for emotional experiences, processing social life and determining reward and punishment, is the first to develop. At this stage, children are more willing to take risks, thus learning what is the possible punishment and what is the reward for specific actions. Only later does the prefrontal cortex, which is responsible for judgment and risk assessment, mature, so teenagers are bigger risk-takers because their prefrontal cortex has not yet developed. Therefore, the child should be allowed to experience the consequences of each action in a natural way (as far as possible), so that he learns to evaluate whether it was pleasant (reward) or not (punishment). If the child's activity is suppressed at this stage, then this part of the brain is underdeveloped, and he himself is unable to evaluate - what is good and what is not. Growing up, he may be afraid, insecure because he has always heard only "can't, can't," but he has never experienced what can really happen.

A little later, and up to about 25 years of age, the part of the brain that is responsible for decision-making, problem-solving, and the ability to perceive complex information develops. That is why puberty is such an important stage, when not only a person's physical appearance changes but also emotional maturity. If a teenager's emotions are suppressed in any way during puberty, over-controlled decision-making, emotional trauma, being in an oppressive environment, or otherwise restricted, it is likely to reverberate in the years to come. I think that's why depression is so common these days. The emotional resistance that arises in us during puberty is the desire to express our true identity - then the brain starts to work in an unprecedented way, and we feel who we want to be. Then a person is ready to create his own identity. However, living in an oppressed society, this opportunity is denied. At the moment when this part of the brain develops, when these neurons start to work - they need to be fired in as many different ways as possible so that we find our best "path." Otherwise, these neural connections do not form properly, and we become confused and easily influenced as adults. Each person has specific character traits, which, yes, are sometimes easily visible already in childhood. But the biggest role is played by which way we direct them and how we develop our brain function in adulthood. When I talk about changing our character, I don't mean simply thinking differently, but physically - how we choose to fire our neurons so that old habits and actions are no longer relevant. How we choose to deal with each new neuron so that it establishes your true identity. This is called neuroplasticity.

When we have not created a strong identity for ourselves, we become "pushed and pushed." We are accustomed to receiving information from the outside, often preprocessed, resembling a synopsis from a volume of ten books, even though in reality, we might have encountered something entirely different in those books. Without crafting our own "summary," we struggle to take responsibility, express an opinion, fear taking risks, and rely on preconceived conclusions, which are not the true path intended for us. In this state, we follow instructions, and yes, it is undoubtedly easier. Acknowledging that the brain tends to be lazy and won't think independently without encouragement, waiting for external judgment becomes a habit. Consequently, we become confused because we lose sight of our desires, making us easily influenced by others' opinions.

When dissatisfied with our lives, it's evident that our earlier decisions were not the best. However, we aren't searching for someone to blame. Whether the decisions were made by us or on our behalf, each choice imparts a lesson, offering an opportunity to realize that there's room for improvement. The question becomes, what else can we do? The subconscious cannot envision something for which you are not prepared. Consider a straightforward example – can you picture yourself living in a skyscraper on the moon? While you might visualize it with effort, it probably wouldn't be your initial thought when envisioning your dream home. When you think about your dream home, you know it's a reflection of what your subconscious desires. Yet, it's simpler to harbor hidden thoughts like "I shouldn't think about a new home all the time" or "I don't deserve it," creating excuses not to pursue it. If you imagine something better than your current situation, it indicates readiness for something more. However, this also implies that you have to take action to attain it – a prospect that some may find daunting.

Sometimes laziness, fear, and ignorance can hinder us from achieving our goals. However, that's why we're here – to overcome the mundane, fortify our significant qualities, and attain what we genuinely desire. It's crucial to be grateful for what we have now, recognizing that our past thoughts have manifested. Yet, it's time to take the next step and discern what else we expect from life. By visualizing and articulating our dreams, we can easily determine the decisions to make in the future, identify habits to change, and ultimately live in alignment with our identity.

To comprehend our true desires, we need to explore various options and understand what we don't want. Therefore, whatever experience we are currently undergoing due to past decisions serves as a valuable guide in realizing our authentic dreams. It's important to recognize that when someone offers advice on decision-making, it's often based on their past experiences and may not align with our actual needs. Therefore, while we appreciate advice and suggestions, it's essential to focus on developing our brains, enabling us to make the best decisions independently and discover what truly suits us

You might wonder, why is change necessary at this moment? Perhaps you frequently feel tired or restless, as if something is consistently catching up with you, and things don't unfold the way you desire. Maybe now you're beginning to sense the desire to listen to yourself, recognizing that your well-being is determined by you, not external conditions. By attaching ourselves to people, activities, and material possessions, we can forget that we are the architects of our own well-being.

Waiting for instructions, seeking permission, or evaluating our lives based on external opinions can make us overlook that the ultimate evaluators are ourselves. Blaming others and incessantly running without introspection is a waste of time. Feelings of dissatisfaction, moodiness, and emptiness are signals urging you to reconcile with yourself. Otherwise, living according to old programs deviates you from your true calling. Life shouldn't be synonymous with suffering or enduring karmic lessons for years. While challenging events may occur, they serve to highlight the contrast and enhance our appreciation for moments of joy.

Currently, the world is transitioning into the new Age of Aquarius. What does this mean? Primarily, people are naturally inclined to seek spiritual development and increased consciousness. The times are changing! Material and physical pursuits are diminishing in value as individuals prioritize their well-being and self-fulfillment. You no longer have to endure life through suffering or work relentlessly for inner peace. Awareness is key – when facing old "karmic" debts, transform yourself to ascend to a "new level."

Karma is no longer resolved through suffering but rather through a deliberate choice to change our usual circumstances. By aligning ourselves with our body and mind, we generate positive vibrations that work through any old 'karmic' tasks, creating space for new possibilities. If a person resists self-love and the desire for transformation, they risk remaining in a state of suffering. Yet, low vibrations are incompatible with the Age of Aquarius, leading to internal conflicts. Transformation becomes imperative. Vibrations are on the rise in the universe, causing time to accelerate. To harmonize with this shift, we must elevate our own vibrations, achievable through self-contentment.

So, what exactly are vibrations? In essence, they are the energy encompassing everything around us, a topic we will explore further. Life becomes remarkably simpler as we step into this new era, nurturing moments of joy and positivity within ourselves. Learning to listen to our inner voice and granting ourselves permission to transform become essential steps.

However, modern society grapples with various addictions—excessive materialism, unhealthy food, alcohol, laziness, and technology. These aren't merely bad habits; for many, they are genuine addictions. Why do people shy away from their passions, opting instead for a monotonous routine? Such a life may feel like suffering, with sentiments of "no one understands me," "I can't do anything," and "everyone else but me" to blame. This reflects crowd psychology, where individuals are accustomed to incessant consumption of goods and content.

A true individual, however, understands their desires and motivations, confident in achieving what is meant for them.

To undergo change is to think, feel, and act in harmony with oneself, ensuring that the created outcomes bring joy to others as well. Essentially, it involves transforming your character and brain function to overcome the barriers of old habits, blocks, and programs that hinder a fulfilling life.

Undoubtedly, this path is more challenging than adhering to familiar programs and societal norms. Yet, as you rewrite your past actions and redefine how others perceive you, you embark on a beautiful journey toward self-improvement and perfection.

What is your ultimate goal? What is your life's calling? Though it may sound cliché, discovering it is crucial. When you start reshaping your thinking and training new neurons, your purpose will reveal itself. Your task is to listen and believe in it. Your essence, soul, or spirit is inherently bright, positive, and joyful—nourish it. Only then will it radiate happiness, passing it on to others.

Your body is a tool, but your essence is paramount. Commence feeding it and relish the fullness of life. Distinguish your logical mind from your intuition; logical thinking is insignificant without intuition's deeper insights. Abandon external programs and craft a life that makes you eager to wake up every day—it's entirely possible!

Before proceeding, a word of caution: the journey may not always be smooth. Personally, I experienced the realization of time wasted living someone else's life—a painful revelation. It's crucial to discard such destructive thoughts swiftly. The past is unchangeable; focus on the present. Your choices now shape your future. The opinions of others become inconsequential when you recognize that the person you must live with forever is yourself.

As you change, your surroundings will shift—inspiring those around you or attracting new connections. Acknowledge that this transformation is for yourself; what you truly need remains, and the irrelevant naturally fades away. If your goal is yet undiscovered, rest assured it leads to an exciting, fulfilling path, culminating in the beautiful, peaceful life you desire.

Before embarking on this journey, dispel myths that claim people don't change or that change is arduous and time-consuming. People can change when they choose to; change isn't inherently difficult, but effective methods must be employed. It doesn't demand a lengthy duration, just a resolute decision to initiate the process. The vibrations you emit will swiftly align with your decisions, ushering in changes promptly.

When embarking on the journey of change, consider these principles:

1 | Be interested in yourself - you must have a genuine desire to comprehend why you act, behave, and think the way you currently do. Self-knowledge is key. Pay particular attention to moments of dissatisfaction and delve into the emotions you experience at those times.

2 | Be open-minded - recognize that there might be barriers preventing you from achieving your goals. If you find yourself discontented with various aspects of your daily life, acknowledge that you haven't yet embraced the best version of yourself. Be receptive to change and self-improvement by incorporating new habits and trying novel experiences.

3 | Don't take anything for granted - refrain from accepting answers such as "It's just the way it is," "Because I was taught that way," or "I can't do it any other way." These are excuses, not genuine explanations. Challenge and discard them.

4 | Don't feel sorry for yourself - formulate direct, open, and probing questions. Imagine yourself as a relentless journalist aiming to uncover hidden truths. Ask the questions you wouldn't want others to ask of you. Be assertive and objective in self-inquiry.

5 | Be open - while it might seem obvious, it's crucial to emphasize the openness principle. Even the "dirty" questions should be answered openly. If needed, engage in a constructive internal dialogue. Challenge yourself with counter-questions to ensure clarity. An open, honest dialogue with yourself reveals areas that require deeper understanding and adjustment.

6 | Don't be afraid of what you hear - sometimes, when you uncover the answers to your questions with complete openness, there might be a moment of resistance. It's normal because learning the truth isn't always pleasant. Regardless, you're the sole possessor of this knowledge. Even if it feels like everyone on the street is staring at you, sensing your secret or problem, remember – you're the only one in the know. This awareness empowers you to resolve and change, ensuring you act differently in the future and avoid repeating past mistakes.

7 | Consult yourself daily - envision approaching your "inner advisor" akin to seeking assistance in a store with a vast array of products. Each day, you can engage in a dialogue like, "Hello, I would like a beautiful, calm day today. Who can make it so?" Your inner response might guide you: "A well-balanced day involves dividing your time between work and activities for self-improvement or health. How about a refreshing walk in the park?" Your response: "Yes, I'm feeling a bit tired, but I don't think I deserve a break yet..." Continue the dialogue: "Don't you deserve a break? How can you recharge to do something positive? Treat yourself to a delicious breakfast, go for a walk, or enjoy a funny movie. Sound like a plan?"

8 | Play! Allow your thoughts to roam freely. The sensation of amusing yourself with internal dialogue is delightful – it's as if you hold a secret that others don't. Embrace it as a game. Become your own best conversational partner. Loneliness doesn't have to be solitude.

WHAT DO YOU NEED TO KNOW
ABOUT YOURSELF

The human nervous system comprises two main parts:

* The central nervous system, consisting of the brain and spinal cord.

* The peripheral nervous system, responsible for transmitting signals from sensory receptors to the spinal cord and brain, as well as conveying signals from the spinal cord and brain to muscles and glands. Neurons, or nerve cells, act as information transmitters between different areas of the brain and the rest of the nervous system. Neurons communicate through neurotransmitters, chemicals transmitted in synapses – small spaces between the dendrites (signal receivers) and axons (carry electrical impulses) of neighboring neurons. When a chemical substance approaches the dendrite of a neighboring neuron, it either excites or inhibits it.

Neuroplasticity involves altering or reprogramming typical neural pathways, resulting in changes in the synapse that either strengthen and increase neural connections or weaken and reduce them. Once neural connections are activated frequently, habits form, leading to automatic actions. Without a conscious effort to break these connections, we continue to act automatically, following old habits. However, since it is possible to change how the brain works by replacing habitual actions with new ones, over time, these "old" pathways can be rewritten, creating new behavioral patterns.

There are approximately 100 different neurotransmitters, or chemicals facilitating communication between neurons.

Key neurotransmitters include serotonin, dopamine, adrenaline, glutamic acid, gamma-aminobutyric acid (GABA), endorphins, histamine, and others. For instance, dopamine not only plays a crucial role in physiological processes but is also linked to psychological conditions, with disruptions in its transmission associated with depression, attention deficit syndrome, schizophrenia, and other psychiatric disorders.

The vagus nerve, one of the body's vital messengers, extends from the brainstem to the abdominal cavity. Despite the common perception that the brain regulates bodily functions, the gut sends more information to the brain than it receives. Since gut microflora utilizes the vagus nerve to communicate with the brain, careful consideration of what and how we eat becomes crucial. This emphasizes the need not only to adopt a complete and balanced diet but also to be mindful of the preparation process and the thoughts associated with it. Understanding that everything consists of energy, with atoms vibrating at different frequencies, is crucial. Just as there can be healthy or unhealthy diets, there are also good or bad vibrations – high frequencies that make you feel good and attract positive events, or low frequencies leading to negative thoughts, fear, anger, and other destructive emotions. Bowel problems can directly impact mental health, causing depression and anxiety, while a healthy gut can contribute to improving emotional states and overall well-being.

The vagus nerve plays a significant role in regulating emotions and managing stressors. It can either reduce stress or increase anxiety and depressive moods, depending on the foods consumed. Various substances and vitamins in food impact the brain and nervous system. For instance, vitamin D, found in eggs, carrots, avocados, and fatty fish, is essential for serotonin production in the brain. Serotonin, along with oxytocin and vasopressin, influences social behavior, and their actions can be influenced by vitamin D levels.

Foods rich in tryptophan, an amino acid present in proteins like milk, eggs, cheese, chicken, oatmeal, and dark chocolate, contribute to serotonin absorption. Adequate vitamin D intake can support serotonin production, leading to an improved mood and better sleep. Conversely, low serotonin levels may result in symptoms such as lack of energy, sadness, mood swings, changes in appetite, sexual dysfunction, sleep difficulties, or excessive sleeping, potentially leading to depression and anxiety.

Dopamine, another crucial neurotransmitter related to motivation and concentration, is produced in a two-step process involving the amino acid tyrosine. Foods like chicken, dairy, bananas, and pumpkins, rich in tyrosine, can help boost dopamine levels. Maintaining a delicate balance between serotonin and dopamine is key to overall well-being, as an imbalance, such as high serotonin and low dopamine, can lead to a content but unmotivated state. Striking this balance contributes to a positive mood and sustained motivation.

What we eat plays a significant role in influencing our feelings, but it's not the sole factor. The vibrations and thoughts of the person preparing the meal also contribute to the overall experience. Our minds are filled with various thoughts, originating from both the conscious and subconscious parts. The subconscious mind, occupying about 95% of our total mind, consists of automatic thoughts and habits formed through repeated experiences.

Thoughts are often derived from past experiences, serving as memories and learned concepts that guide our future actions. However, if past experiences have been distressing, they can affect our present mindset, leading us to unknowingly hold onto outdated information. It's crucial to realize that what happened in the past does not dictate the present. Failing to be present in the moment can lead to cultivating destructive thoughts, creating low vibrations within ourselves, and inadvertently spreading negativity.

The universe operates on energy, and everything, including thoughts, is a form of energy. As the Earth transitions into the Age of Aquarius, vibrations are rapidly increasing. Living in low vibrations, characterized by fear, power struggles, suffering, and control, is no longer suitable. To align with the higher vibrations of the new era, individuals must elevate their own atomic vibrations. This alignment brings forth qualities like joy, love, gratitude, and inspiration.

Our thoughts shape our energy field, creating an electro-magnetic field around us that influences what we attract in the future. When thoughts are filled with fear, shame, or negativity, the energy within us can become heavy. Acting through the ego and resisting change can result in discomfort, emphasizing the importance of aligning thoughts with higher vibrations for a more positive and fulfilling life.

Change your thinking and break free from the shackles of past events. The past is no longer tangible; it exists only in memories. Embrace the present moment, as it is the only reality you have right now. Dwelling on painful memories can plunge you into low emotions, potentially attracting more negative events. Instead, view challenging experiences as valuable lessons, transforming them into opportunities for gratitude and appreciation for the present.

Gratitude is a powerful force that elevates your vibrations and attracts positivity. Take a moment to acknowledge and be thankful for what you currently have. By cultivating gratitude, you create an environment of abundance, inviting new positive experiences and people into your life. Embrace the power of positive thought, and witness the transformative impact on your everyday life.

Now, let's delve into the intricate connection between your body and mind. Ever experienced a lump in your throat due to unspoken words or fallen ill just before a significant event? Our bodies are not mere machines; they are intricately linked to our thoughts and emotions. Prolonged stress or new-found inner peace can alter the body by changing thought patterns. The body is a holistic system, with energy centers associated with various organs, each having its own mental aspect. Thoughts significantly influence these energy centers, impacting their normal functioning.

When an energy center is blocked, it restricts the free flow of energy, leading to issues in the corresponding area. For instance, a blocked energy center related to trust might hinder the establishment of new relationships. Identifying and addressing these blocks is crucial for restoring the natural flow of energy. Whether referred to as blocked energy, composed energy, or closed chakras, the underlying principle remains the same – free-flowing energy is essential for the overall well-being of the body and mind. Just as good nutrition is vital, cultivating positive thoughts is equally essential for promoting a healthy and balanced life.

Your identity is an intricate interplay of various elements, including the nervous system, electromagnetic field, and energy centers. These components serve as the primary tools for embarking on the journey of personal development and cultivating qualities that lead to fulfillment. By understanding and working with these tools, you can take deliberate steps towards positive change.

The nervous system, responsible for transmitting signals between the brain and the rest of the body, plays a crucial role in your responses and behaviors. The electromagnetic field generated by your thoughts creates an invisible but powerful force that influences your experiences and interactions. Additionally, the energy centers, associated with different aspects of your being, reflect the holistic connection between your body and mind.

Embarking on the path of self-improvement doesn't necessarily require a complete life overhaul. Even small changes within yourself can bring about a profound shift, allowing you to perceive your existing life in new and vibrant colors. Life is inherently beautiful and simple, and by actively shaping it according to your desires, you have the power to create the life you truly want.

MAJOR AND MINOR QUALITIES

In the journey of personal development, qualities can be categorized into large and small characteristics. The large qualities are pivotal, defining our overall well-being, personal growth, and how we interact with others. Strengthening these qualities is a primary task, as it allows us to reach our natural state where we feel most aligned with our true selves. By developing these great qualities, we can overcome fears, envy, and other unnatural states caused by past traumas, enabling us to act authentically.

On the other hand, small qualities serve as supportive mechanisms and help maintain the big ones. Although their importance is sometimes underestimated or not fully understood, these small characteristics play a crucial role in our everyday lives. While they may not directly build the larger qualities, they contribute to the stability and longevity of these significant attributes. To use an analogy, they are like the interior design after the house is built or the clothing on the fabric.

In society, there is often less emphasis on the development of great qualities, as individual thinking may not conform to crowd psychology. However, focusing on these major qualities is essential for building a solid foundation for personal growth. To draw a parallel, nothing lasting can be built on weak or non-existent foundations. Therefore, it is advisable to prioritize the development of large qualities before delving into the improvement of smaller ones.

Understanding the harmony between small and large properties involves recognizing their sequential nature, akin to building a house before designing its interior. Often, as we grow up, we may not be informed about the real need for certain qualities, and habits develop without a full understanding of their underlying reasons. Realizing this in adulthood empowers us to question ingrained thoughts and beliefs, allowing us to be true to ourselves.

Acting in alignment with our true nature may sometimes contradict what we were taught, leading to feelings of guilt or the fear of not meeting expectations. In these moments, recognizing the conflict with our intuition can guide us towards understanding and embracing our authentic selves. It's an opportunity for self-discovery, paving the way for personal growth and a more genuine, fulfilling life.

I do not aim to condemn anyone for imperfect upbringing, and this book is not about that. It's crucial to understand that everyone did their best based on what they knew. I am genuinely grateful for the efforts my parents put in, and that's why I mentioned at the beginning of the book that, after high school, I struggled with the responsibilities of adult life. Now, taking charge of my own life, I've learned extensively to align with the kind of life I desire and to become a more pleasant version of myself.

Observing individuals who are free, happy, and possess their own identity, I noticed commonalities among them. While not exactly identical in each person, certain characteristics stood out: Responsibility. Courage. Empathy. Respect. The big four. The foundation for greatness. These qualities, upon reflection, revealed themselves as traits that cannot be acquired from external sources; they require internal work. They serve as the main steps toward achieving the life you dream of, constructing an identity so robust that everyday life becomes easy and pleasant.

I am grateful to myself for following this path and finding the peace I yearned for over the past 10 years. My greatest hope is that every person reading this book feels as good as I do right now, if not better. Admittedly, there are still situations that can throw me off, but I consider them trifles. In those moments, I quickly recognize that they occur to further strengthen my big four and discover optimal ways to enhance my natural state.

Embarking on the journey to becoming the best version of yourself, remember that this change is for your benefit. Even if your initial motivation is self-driven, as you evolve, various thoughts and situations may arise, tempting you back to the old "version." Be cautious of those who believe they have power over you. Understand that people's brains can be both polluted and lazy; they prefer not to rethink what has already been considered. Contrary to the belief that first impressions are most important, it's vital to recognize the ever-changing nature of people. Convincing your closest associates that you've changed or are on the path to change can be challenging. There will be moments when you ponder, "I have changed! What more must I do to be treated differently?" The answer is simple: change should be for yourself, not for others. Inner awareness is key – knowing that this time, you'll react differently because you've already changed. Life's challenges, often perceived as tests, prompt negative reactions. Consider them lessons, repeating until they solidify your transformation. If a situation offends or angers you, recognize that the issue lies not in the other person or the specific event but in the emotions it triggers within you.

Absolutely, it's not specific individuals who provoke our anger or offense, but rather the emotions triggered by their actions or words. These actions often evoke memories from the past. Until we thoroughly understand the memories associated with these sensations, we'll continue to encounter these 'teaching' moments. Becoming aware of what hurt you in the past, identifying what was said and why it made you feel a certain way, allows you to consciously recognize that your reaction is not to the current situations, but to the past injury.

Hence, it's crucial to remember that on the path of self-development, you don't have to prove anything to anyone but yourself. The transformation is for your benefit. Recognition from others is not a prerequisite. Those content with themselves, or at least on the way to it, will notice because they comprehend the process of change, breaking old habits, and shedding outdated behavior patterns and stereotypes.

The most significant reward lies in the sense of improvement. Confidence will surge within you, bringing a profound sense of peace. You'll be pleasantly surprised to find that the things that used to worry you are now minor concerns that fade with time. Even if you experience moments of anger or sadness, you'll recognize them as normal emotions, acknowledging that everyone experiences them. Refrain from self-judgment or blame; altering oneself requires effort but stands as the greatest gift for long-term well-being. Protect this gift from anyone trying to diminish its value, for you deserve to shape the life you desire. Engage in the substantial work on yourself, and now is the opportune moment to delve into the discussion of the first significant quality and the techniques to cultivate it.

GROW UP!

Have you ever viewed your parents through the eyes of a child, taking everything they did for granted? The preparation of meals, family outings, clothing purchases—all regarded as ordinary, self-evident occurrences. Many children, and even adults, fall into the trap of perceiving these actions as commonplace while simultaneously allowing themselves to be held responsible for things left undone. This inclination can be labeled as indulgence, defined as "to harm character by being excessively lenient or permissive." Paradoxically, boundless giving and permissiveness may inflict more harm than good on a child's character. Excessive indulgence can result in the gradual loss of the feeling of joy, both for the child and the eventual adult.

Consider this scenario: if you were to receive your favorite meal every day for lunch, how long would the enjoyment last? Continuous pampering and indulgence have the potential to transform individuals into endlessly demanding people who lose touch with their desires and struggle to accept rejection, often blaming others. This perpetual pampering may also foster narcissistic traits, impacting not only the individual, often unknowingly, but also their new family, subject to unexplained selfish impulses and demands.

When discussing the pitfalls of spoiling and taking things for granted, it's crucial to remember that nothing should be assumed or taken lightly. Every action performed by parents or any other close individual should be acknowledged and appreciated. Every incident that has caused hurt requires self-resolution, sooner or later. No one else should bear the blame—it's a personal journey of recognition and forgiveness. By doing so, you pave the way to construct your life as you desire. It is unjust to lay the blame on the person who made the mistake. The expectations were yours, and if they were not met, why hold someone else responsible? The only solution is to commence taking responsibility!

Responsibility, in essence, is the capacity to identify the optimal solution and undertake appropriate actions to enhance a situation or circumstance, ensuring it does not leave a negative impact on others.

FORMS OF RESPONSIBILITY

There are four dimensions of responsibility – body, mind, energy, and spirit. As human beings, owners of bodies, and bearers of souls, we must strive to maintain these aspects in optimal order throughout our lives.

Body – Biological (nutrition, brain health, sleep, sports, etc.).
Mind – Psychological (inner speech, trauma, upbringing, blocks, thought forms).
Energy (Field) – Social (environment, relationships, family, friends, connection).
Spirit - Spiritual (calling, higher purpose, inspiration, values, beliefs, intuition, feeding the soul).

During a child's exploration of the world, mistakes are frequently made. The limbic system, responsible for evaluating reward and punishment, develops several years before the frontal cortex, which is in charge of decision-making. Often, children hear phrases like "don't do that," imprinting specific thought forms without necessarily promoting the development of the frontal cortex for independent decision-making. Learning from mistakes is a valuable aspect of growth. While we may not predict when or how we'll make a mistake, analyzing each mistake enables us to become wiser with every experience and prepares us to approach things differently in the future.

However, our minds often echo with "don't" or "don't do that!" without fostering the growth of independent decision-making. While parental concerns for a child's safety are valid, disallowing mistakes in minor matters prevents the child from learning to assess what is beneficial for them. Your identity takes shape within your family, influenced by the perspectives of two individuals on what is good and right. Over the years, when faced with reluctance or fear, using "I was raised that way" as an excuse becomes common. While acknowledging this upbringing is your responsibility, it's crucial to learn and develop your authentic identity. You can make this decision at any moment when you realize that your current way of life no longer serves you.

Every person harbors unique interests, desires, and abilities. People are inherently diverse. Remaining confined to thought forms established in childhood may lead to a less-than-ideal life experience. Imagine if your parents raised you within the context of their lives, shielding you from making mistakes. If such actions, deemed errors, diminish continually, what is left in the end? Childhood experiences of 'punishment' and 'reward' (mistakes and successes) are instrumental in learning responsibility.

Many daily activities are performed unconsciously, hindering development. Recognizing and changing these aspects require taking responsibility for oneself. Subconsciously, many have internalized the notion that self-improvement is challenging. Consider the stereotypes—getting up early is difficult, eating healthy is expensive and time-consuming, good clothes require a hefty income, living beautifully necessitates hard work, looking beautiful requires a high income, and the list goes on. Excuses for everything abound, often ingrained subconsciously by external influences, preventing us from questioning their validity. Many of these stereotypes aren't based on personal experiences.

The "bullying" and programming that occurred over time have hindered your ability to take responsibility for yourself. However, through creating your own experiences, you will learn to discern genuine advice from attempts to suppress your desire to achieve your goals. Genuine advice is a rarity and is rooted in the best outcome for you given the specific circumstances. Someone who has been in a similar situation – at a particular age, time, gender, and economic situation – can offer valuable advice on how to navigate challenges. True advice often takes the form of questions rather than statements, helping you uncover your priorities and desired results.

Formed habits can be challenging to recognize, as they were often established with the assumption that they would be better or easier for you. However, exploring uncharted paths might reveal more suitable and efficient alternatives. To foster responsibility, it's crucial to delve deeper into the four forms of responsibility.

Bodily responsibility, or biological responsibility, is widely discussed today. Topics such as healthy eating, sports, and sleep have been extensively researched, providing ample information for the public. It's essential to explore various perspectives and find an approach that suits individual needs. Biological responsibility extends beyond mere physical care, involving a deeper understanding of your body's needs and the best ways to enhance its well-being. It's about respecting and loving your body, not just adhering to doctor visits and prescribed medicines. The activities you engage in to maintain physical fitness are interconnected with your thoughts about food, self-image, and overall mental well-being. Negative thoughts often stem from subconscious programs. Reflecting on your daily thoughts is essential for understanding your mental landscape.

If bodily responsibility gained popularity with the rise of fast-food establishments worldwide, psychological responsibility, or caring for one's mind, is currently experiencing a surge in popularity. The mind comprises the conscious and the subconscious, with the subconscious accounting for about 95% of the entire mind. Cleaning the subconscious of unnecessary clutter is crucial since it influences who you aspire to be and what you attract into your life. Remember, your thoughts shape your reality, so it's essential to choose your thoughts wisely.

Thinking correctly is a fundamental aspect of psychological responsibility, and here are some guiding principles:

- Accurate thoughts involve knowing what you want, planning your actions and life, envisioning the desired outcome, and choosing the right people around you.

- Positive thoughts contribute to a good mood, lightness, health, and a positive outlook on your surroundings.

- Productive thoughts are followed by action; you actively seek opportunities to fulfill your intentions and focus on implementing plans rather than dwelling on "what if" scenarios.

- Better less is about quality over quantity; it's better to have fewer positive thoughts than a surplus of mediocre ones.

To achieve this, practice self-control. Recognize that constant thinking is unnecessary, and allow your mind to relax by diverting your thoughts to positive activities like listening to music, reading, meditating, or cooking. Avoid creating problems where none exist and be present in the moment to prevent your mind from wandering into unnecessary and inhibiting fictional scenarios.

Maintaining clear and positive thoughts extends to what you expose yourself to—what you listen to, watch, and surround yourself with. This leads to the third form of responsibility—energy. Your environment significantly impacts your thoughts, and if your energy isn't sufficiently strengthened, external influences can easily throw you off course. Focus your energy so strongly that external factors cannot disrupt it. Your energy determines what you attract into your life, adhering to the principles of physics. The following section will elaborate on the physics laws introduced earlier.

The body, like everything else, is composed of atoms in a constant state of vibration. Within the body, there are several energy centers, each with distinct biological structures—comprising glands, hormones, chemicals, and individual "brains." Consequently, each energy center possesses its own mind. When a person has a thought, it triggers physiological changes in the body, influencing the energy. The mind in the brain influences the mind in the body, operating at a subconscious level through the autonomic nervous system. If negative past experiences are stored in the subconscious, these energy centers can become blocked, hindering the free flow of energy and causing stagnation.

There are eight primary energy centers:

1. The first center governs the genital area, associated with reproduction and sexuality, containing a significant amount of creative energy.

2. The second center, located behind and slightly below the navel, controls organs like the ovaries, uterus, colon, pancreas,

and lower back. It is linked to relationships, family, and culture, fostering feelings of freedom and safety when in balance.

3. The third energy center in the solar plexus area regulates organs like the stomach, small intestine, spleen, liver, gall bladder, adrenal glands, and kidneys. It relates to human will, power, control, inner drive, aggression, and dominance, responsible for personal power and self-esteem.

4. The fourth center, behind the sternum, oversees the heart, lungs, and thymus. It marks the transition from selfishness to selflessness, embodying love, care, gratitude, inspiration, kindness, and trust. In balance, one feels love for life and contentment.

5. The fifth energy center in the throat controls the thyroid, salivary glands, and neck tissues. It is associated with truthful expression, constructing reality through language and sound. Balance leads to satisfaction, truthful communication, and sharing thoughts and feelings willingly.

6. The sixth center, located in the center of the brain, controls the pineal gland, aiding in non-linear reality perception. It enables clear thinking, consciousness, and heightened awareness.

7. The seventh center in the head harmonizes and connects downward to other centers, bringing overall balance. Harmony prevails when this center is balanced.

8. The eighth energy center, situated approximately 40 cm above the head, symbolizes a connection with the whole. Activation brings perfection, generosity, revelations, an understanding of life, and the ability to perceive information beyond stored memories in the nervous system.

If energy becomes stagnant, it impedes free development. For instance, if someone has been conditioned since childhood to believe that sex is bad, the energy may become trapped in the first center, hindering the individual from expressing their creative potential. Similarly, experiences of betrayal or trauma can cause energy blockages in the second center, leading to issues such as low self-esteem, guilt, shame, and difficulty letting go of the past. When energy is confined to the third center, it can result in complications with the ego, leading to excessive control, dominance, and anger. The majority of energy blockages occur in the first three centers, restricting the flow of the higher five, which are crucial for experiencing genuine love for life.

Each energy center vibrates at its unique frequency, and when a center is blocked, its frequency diminishes. The weakening of signal frequencies can attract illness, as the organism no longer receives complete information from the affected center, impairing its proper functioning. On the other hand, atoms with similar vibrations bond together, sharing energy and information to form molecules. As more atoms join, a chemical substance is created, which can further evolve into a cell. When groups of cells unite, tissues are formed, and when several tissues combine, organs are created, each containing a field of energy and information that supports healthy functioning.

In summary, the human body is a complex chain starting from thoughts, environment, people, and consumed media. Clearing the subconscious mind is crucial for balancing energy centers. Your surroundings, interactions, and media consumption significantly influence your thinking, either aiding in your development or hindering it. If you find an area where change seems elusive or you feel stuck, addressing your subconscious programs becomes a priority. This effort can foster energy balance, enabling unhindered development in the future. In essence, raising your vibrations is key because your vibrational frequency determines what you attract. Challenge yourself to think beyond your current environment, surround yourself with positive influences, and be mindful of the vibrations that shape whether you live in suffering and conflict or in gratitude, fulfilling your desires. Empower yourself to change outdated thought patterns and take responsibility for ensuring that you, and no one else, control your energy.

If energy responsibility can be likened to physics, the fourth form of responsibility takes on a more ethereal nature. It involves responsibility to one's spirit, or self-inspiration. What truly brings you happiness? What provides you with a sense of fulfillment? Is it the sight of something beautiful, the melody of good music, or the enjoyment of your favorite food? When do you experience that inner, pleasant tingle?

Spiritual fulfillment is a feeling—an emotion that brings us joy. It's not tied to a specific thing but is rather a sensation that uplifts us. It's essential to recognize that seeking happiness solely in pleasures may gradually numb our senses over time. Pleasures offer short-term gratification, not enduring happiness. However, within those moments of joy lies something that truly nourishes you. Sensation is a psychic process reflecting stimuli acting on sense organ receptors. Most organic sensations are linked to the functioning of various nerve centers in the brain, providing physical proof that happiness isn't confined to physical pleasures. So, where is it found? Considering happiness as satisfaction with life, purpose, and meaning, how can we attain it?

Take notice of what makes you feel your best. Do you often listen to your intuition, following impulses that might seem unconventional but are irresistible? Reflect on activities you enjoyed as a child—those untainted by adult constraints like "it's not appropriate" or "you can't make money with it." What you did in childhood often aligns with your true purpose or natural talent, a gift meant to be developed in this life. By expressing your natural talent, you contribute positively to others, fostering a mutually beneficial exchange. In childhood, before logic and traumas impact us, our inner voice is loud and clear. Parents play a vital role in recognizing and encouraging these early interests. When choices are dictated by others, suppressing intuition can lead to burnout and depression. Fulfillment comes when you engage in activities with enthusiasm, passion, and inspiration—especially when they benefit society, regardless of financial gain. It's that feeling when talking or thinking about your passion gives you goosebumps or butterflies, an excitement that transcends monetary concerns. Discovering one's highest purpose is unique for each person. Embrace that passion, share your talents, and you're on the path to personal and societal enrichment—an excellent way to quickly assume responsibility for your spirit and nourish it!

When contemplating all four forms of responsibility—body, mind, energy, spirit—the key is understanding how you wish to define yourself in three main aspects. Do you envision yourself as healthy, sporty, and active? Perhaps calm, creative, and logical? Maybe generous, present, and in balance? Initiating self-responsibility begins with crafting a vision of who you want to be today, tomorrow, and in the next ten years.

Think in reverse—identify moments when you feel discomfort or unease. Is it when carrying groceries or climbing to the 5th floor? If so, prioritize physical fitness. Is it when interacting with strangers? Then work on improving your communication skills. Consider how you'd like to feel in these "uncomfortable" situations. If frequent travel is in your future, prepare by strengthening yourself for carrying luggage or learn basic phrases in different languages for solo travel comfort[3]. You can develop any aspect you perceive as a weakness, and it doesn't have to involve complex fitness plans or top-tier online courses. To begin being more physically active, start with simple stretches in the morning, a lap around the stadium, or even a single push-up. It's these small steps that signal a shift in your mindset, proving that change can be straightforward!

Now that you're acquainted with all four forms of responsibility and understand their significance in personal development, you can embark on this journey. Remember, no one else will do it for you, and that's a positive aspect. It empowers you to design yourself precisely the way you want. While it may sound appealing, what does it truly entail to become accountable to yourself?

WHAT IT TAKES TO BE RESPONSIBLE

One might ponder why responsibility stands out as a great quality and what would ensue if we were not responsible. In my perspective, lacking responsibility renders life akin to a squirrel's wheel—often complained about, where it seems everything is in place, yet nothing substantial unfolds. It's like running somewhere but getting nowhere—a perpetual loop with no clear exit. Do we not wish to break free, or perhaps, are we simply not taking any meaningful action?

Being responsible to oneself, one's goals, and social life necessitates the cultivation of self-discipline. In essence, what dissatisfies you is often the outcome of insufficient self-discipline. Satisfaction can only be attained when the requisite time and effort are invested in achieving your goals.

Responsibility involves either accepting circumstances without complaint or taking the initiative to mold them to align with your desires—be it your income, body, health, appearance, or daily life. Every aspect can be enhanced to approach your ideal, reducing elements that dissatisfy or hinder your progress. Elevating responsibility in your life, contributing to your well-being, primarily demands responsibility towards yourself, underpinned by significant self-discipline. This forms a solid foundation for all aspects of your future life.

If you cannot master responsibility for yourself, it becomes challenging to extend responsibility to others. How can you assist someone else if your own life is not in order? To offer support, you must first achieve fulfillment yourself. While it might sound logical, the common tendency is to give endlessly until realizing emptiness, neglecting self-fulfillment. Others may label it as service or self-sacrifice, believing that by helping others, one will receive in return. However, this is contingent on disciplined self-care and responsibility.

Discipline hinges on transforming habits. Often, life's potential goes untapped due to habitual actions echoing in our minds: "Do what you're accustomed to!" "Follow others' directives!" "Go where you are welcomed, not where you desire!" Habits are actions performed so frequently that they become automatic, and the brain tends to adhere to them. However, creating something new and breaking old behavioral patterns is essential for personal transformation. Consistently engaging in the familiar confines us to a predictable existence. Embracing the unplanned, unexpected, and unfamiliar can instantly reshape our future, drawing in new opportunities in life.

Discipline arises from mastering your mind and comprehending its functioning. Once you discern how your thoughts operate and identify the excuses they generate, you gain the upper hand, enabling you to anticipate them and modify your customary actions. Initiate the process by contemplating the visible factors that consistently consume your time. Do you believe there are numerous such elements? Record every activity you engaged in today or yesterday, including seemingly trivial occurrences (like conversing with a neighbor, waiting in line at the store, etc.). Document time-consuming elements, individuals, devices, and habits, and estimate the time allocated to each. Contemplate how much of your energy and time is being expended unnecessarily. Now, I encourage you to consider: "Let them go!" Will you take that step?

WHY IS IT SO HARD?

Why do we find it challenging to motivate ourselves? Why is it often easier to conjure up reasons not to take action than to make the decision to start and figure out the best approach? It's crucial to recall that only about 5% of our actions are performed consciously—meaning, with deliberate thought. The remaining 95% occur mechanically, akin to programmed robots. This is why the saying goes, "Once you've learned to ride a bike, you'll know it for the rest of your life." Certainly, the subconscious mind has its positive aspects. Once we've learned and practiced something sufficiently, we don't need to relearn it each time.

Consider the analogy of learning to drive a car. Initially, the actions required felt like a mental exercise, coordinating limbs and attention. However, after repeated practice, these actions become automatic, stored in the deepest recesses of the brain. Buckling up and shifting gears become second nature

Now, how does this relate to discipline? The mind tends to avoid excessive thinking; it prefers habits. The brain is inherently lazy and leans towards creating automatic routines. While there are certainly beneficial habits that enhance our daily lives, creating and developing them demands self-discipline or, more simply, "getting along." To facilitate their adoption, the mind needs to anticipate the rewards following these actions. Habits often form when we know a reward will follow a specific action, providing immediate gratification. Breaking bad habits is challenging because they offer immediate pleasures—junk food, for instance—while good habits, like healthy eating, reward us with long-term benefits, such as improved health and a great physique.

Despite the difficulty in erasing old habits, we can replace them with new ones. A habit is built upon a "signal" that triggers action. For instance, coming home might signal a trip to the fridge. It's essential to find an alternative positive activity for that signal—maybe taking a shower upon arriving home or putting on your sports shoes for a 10-minute walk immediately upon waking up. When establishing a new habit, begin with the easiest form possible to convey to the mind that it's not overly challenging. Additionally, devise a reward for yourself, such as applying a pleasant cream after a shower or savoring a long-desired coffee after a morning walk or run. Soon, you'll discover that the fresh morning air during a run wakes you up better than coffee. Drinking coffee immediately after waking disrupts the natural development of dopamine, the key to motivation and the desire for a reward. Opting for a more gradual approach allows the body to produce dopamine naturally, ensuring sustained motivation.

Eating fruits, getting healthy sleep, and breathing fresh air are, of course, some of the best ways to help the brain rest and stay fit. However, in my experience, if the mind is overwhelmed with thoughts, leading to anxiety or depressive feelings, exercise is definitely the best remedy. You don't need much—just a focused 30-minute workout a day is quite enough. This includes a walk around the city; walking at a leisurely pace counts as a workout. Running, cycling, or going to the gym are also good options. It is important to be focused on a specific activity at that moment and be present in it. Feel how the body works and inhale fresh wind through the nose. Deep breaths through the nose allow you to take in a large amount of energy since the air contains substances necessary for the human body.

When I started running, I aimed to focus on as few goals as possible for faster achievement. That's exactly what I think about small goals—I only need to run one lap around the stadium, and then I can start listening to music and reward myself with other milestones. When the mind stops dwelling on how hard it is and feels every cell in the whole body in motion, and the accumulated energy is revived, this is the greatest reward. The strangest thing is that when you realize that running or other physical activity doesn't tire you but actually recharges you, then next time you know better that you need to train your mind more than your body. It's so interesting. Any physical activity can be liked. The main thing is to start with very small steps so that you feel the reward faster, and the mind begins to remember this as a pleasant activity.

INFLUENCE

Little by little, we begin to understand how easy it is to create a new habit. Now, let's try to recall how many of the recent actions you've taken were solely your choice. Can you identify the last thing you did based on your beliefs and desires without any external factors influencing your choice? Think carefully. Even if it was something small, consider the reasons behind your actions. For instance, what were your last purchases? What news did you read? How did you spend yesterday? Were all the tasks you completed chosen by you? How do you plan to organize your tomorrow?

I used to have a tendency to help anyone who asked, attend events where I was invited, and ultimately neglect my own desires. Don't get me wrong; helping people and attending events are positive actions, but they need to be prioritized. I learned to evaluate whether my assistance was sought for my abilities and talents or merely because I was an "easy target." Similarly, I questioned if my presence was desired because of my personality or simply to spare someone from going alone. Consider the areas where others try to influence you and why you acquiesce to their influence.

Every day, we come under the influence of someone. One basic rule of influence is: if you want someone to act in your favor, give them what they want. This sounds fair—receiving something in return. However, problems arise when it contradicts your values and the plans you have for the day. Without planning our daily lives, it's easy to be "pushed" into following someone else's agenda. It's even worse if we allow ourselves to be manipulated, canceling our plans because we're enticed or persuaded into supposedly better options. Self-discipline and character strength are essential prerequisites for taking responsibility for your life.

Why do people seek to influence others? Most often, it's because they lack self-assurance and fear acting alone, as that would entail taking responsibility for their actions. Many people avoid going to concerts, theaters, or cafes alone and find it challenging to travel solo. Not everyone follows this pattern, but the societal norm often dictates that you should always have company. The fear of being perceived as a loner or being bored can easily make us lose our individuality. If we constantly need company for our activities, we lack confidence in ourselves. If we always respond to others' invitations, we exclude activities that truly align with our preferences. Consistently responding to others' invitations signals that we are easily influenced, leading to more invitations for activities that may not align with our identity. The fear of rejection or being forgotten may push us to agree to things that consume not only our free time but also a significant amount of energy. This energy could be invested in more meaningful pursuits that actually enhance, rather than deplete, our energy levels.

Frequently, such influence emanates from those closest to you, who have already turned routine into habit - meeting because it's an expectation, helping because it's a given, eating because someone readily provides. This influence often slips by unnoticed, seamlessly becoming a habit that we automatically comply with, seldom questioning our actions. So, why do we allow ourselves to be influenced? Because it's undeniably easier! It's simpler not to engage in independent thought.

It's consistently more convenient not to think but to depend on the inventions of others. I'm referring to minor everyday occurrences as well as substantial ones - this is why most of us don't attempt to invent a new phone or wheel but opt to purchase the ones already invented and mass-produced. Hence, it is more convenient to "scroll" through the phone because you don't have to contemplate what interesting and new things you'd like to know or learn. Similarly, it is more straightforward to follow the latest fashion trends than to craft your own distinctive style. The possibilities for such examples are boundless. Consequently, I pose a question to myself from now on - am I acting based on my own ideas and desires, or am I unknowingly yielding to external influence?

WHAT DOES IT MEAN IF THERE IS
A LACK OF RESPONSIBILITY

Honestly, the first thing that comes to mind when considering a lack of responsibility and a failure to develop self-discipline is boredom. In my view, this is the primary factor that renders life incomplete. Of course, one might question what constitutes boredom. Is routine inherently tedious? If it's a choice you've made and crafted to align with your preferences, it doesn't necessarily have to be mundane. Routine is subjective, embodying an individual's pace and unique actions. For someone, frequent business trips abroad might be routine, while for another, it could be perceived as an exclusive way of life. However, a monotonous life characterized by the cycle of "home-work-home-TV-bed" might indeed resemble a routine bordering on boredom. My point is that infusing elements like physical activity, scheduled events, small goals related to healthy habits, or acquiring new skills into your routine can inject vibrancy into your day, presenting numerous opportunities for enrichment. Gradually, the conventional 9-to-5 workday may not seem as monotonous, as the rest of your time becomes enriched with positive experiences. You leverage your skills without feeling drained because fulfillment is found in other aspects of your life.

In reality, exhaustion sets in when we fail to replenish ourselves adequately. This applies not only to work but also to relationships, home life, and every aspect of our existence. Routine alone cannot rejuvenate us. Recharging must be a deliberate act fueled by the desire to do so, as we are the sole arbiters of what we need in any given moment. A simple bath may work wonders on occasion, while other times, a two-day weekend hike may be the solution. Recharging needs to be woven into your routine. By taking small daily steps, you're likely to quickly forget what burnout feels like. This forms one of the initial requirements for being responsible to yourself — diversifying your daily life to prevent the body, mind, energy, and spirit from succumbing to routine fatigue and nurturing them by cultivating self-discipline and new habits. Take charge of creating your unique routine!

Believe me, the only limitations are those imposed by your mind and the reluctance to live life on your terms. No "right" moment or person will appear unless you take the initiative. Interestingly, as you start taking action, you'll discover that you already possess everything you need. Fear of making mistakes, fear of judgment for not conforming to expectations, fear of losing someone from your life due to your authentic actions — embrace it all! Unnecessary elements will naturally fade away, making room for those that align with your new lifestyle, enhancing your everyday experience. Don't fear loss; fear becoming entangled in boredom and antiquated thinking. Once you redirect your focus to who you genuinely want to be, the only obstacle is your mindset, not the external circumstances.

FEAR OF RESPONSIBILITY

The fear of taking responsibility, known as hypengiophobia, often manifests as significant stress and anxiety, even at the mere thought of responsibility. This fear frequently originates in childhood, where exhibiting initiative to parents or peers led to ridicule, or conversely, where a child was consistently guided and made decisions for, inhibiting the development of independent thinking and responsibility. Unfortunately, these patterns often persist into adulthood, manifesting as a fear of commitment, reluctance to change careers, or hesitation to relocate. How do you confront these fears? Are you adept at handling them independently, or do you seek constant guidance? What kind of life and family do you envision creating, and can you recognize the innate power within you to shape it in a way that future generations will cherish?

Realize that you possess the ability to create something enduring, something with lasting value that benefits society and leaves a positive memory of you.

Your primary task now is to embrace this responsibility wholeheartedly, with genuine intent.

Don't hesitate to establish new traditions. Reflect on your current traditions—Christmas dinners, Easter egg painting. Why do you follow these practices? Are they rooted in your religious beliefs, or are they simply habits ingrained in your surroundings, inherited from parents, neighbors, or friends? While not intending to disrupt your usual celebrations, consider the essence of these activities. Do you spend the summer solstice night without sleep, welcoming the Sun's energy?

During Christmas, do you reflect on religious significance or focus more on Santa Claus? Understand the reasons behind your celebrations, your beliefs, and contemplate the habits you want to pass on to the next generation—whether you'll perpetuate those inherited or introduce new values.

You are the architect of your life and the foundation for your family's future. Yes, you continue what was started, but without introducing innovation, family traditions risk becoming increasingly bare. The emphasis on family continuity and tradition is intentional—illustrating how trivial daily habits can be. You have the potential to create something significant, but the struggle with small habits persists due to a lack of self-discipline. It's time to broaden your perspective and realize that taking responsibility for your body, mind, energy, and spirit is just the beginning. Greater, more crucial, and more responsible tasks await—and that's truly exciting!

Shame and guilt often act as barriers to taking responsibility. The shame of making mistakes or the guilt associated with altering or abandoning familiar routines out of respect for your parents can be powerful deterrents. However, remember that you alone live your life. Your task is not to cling to the old for the sake of it, but to make improvements aligned with your beliefs. Prioritize yourself, create a legacy based on your convictions, adhere to your values, and establish meaningful traditions that offer genuine interest—not just for gatherings and gift exchanges, but for the added value they bring. Strive for balance—recognize the importance of drawing from your ancestors while appreciating the value you can contribute. Both aspects are equally crucial, but your responsibility lies in evaluating their significance rather than rigidly adhering to the old.

A person who avoids responsibility often lacks confidence in themselves and their abilities, undermining their own actions. This lack of faith can lead to self-torment through the creation of various scenarios predicting negative outcomes for their actions. Such thinking is baseless. There is no person who has done everything wrong. Even when viewed through a narrow "right-wrong" scale, an understanding of probability theory reveals that, sooner or later, even when "shooting blindly," one will hit the target. Therefore, it's essential to adopt a more relaxed approach to life.

Parents frequently instill fear in their children about potential abandonment in adulthood, leading to an incomplete cultivation of "big thinking," determination to act, and the ability to learn from mistakes. This upbringing can contribute to a lack of desire to take responsibility, turning a natural aspect of life into an unnecessarily serious matter. Taking responsibility should be seen more as a game than a burden.

Here are some common reasons, whether conscious or unconscious, that hinder the acceptance of responsibility:

Lack of experience - Individuals who shy away from responsibility often haven't faced it enough times. It's crucial to practice making decisions regularly. Just as it takes approximately 10,000 hours of practice to developa new skill, the same principle applies to taking responsibility. Regular training can normalize it, making it a natural and self-evident state as the initial excitement fades. Remember, we excel at what we've done before, so consistent practice is key.

2 | Bad experience and failure - if you've attempted to take responsibility in the past and experienced failure, view it as a valuable learning opportunity. Rather than succumbing to reproaches or playing the victim, understand where you went wrong and use that knowledge to approach situations differently next time. It's always easier to rectify your own mistakes than those made by someone else. Embrace failure as a stepping stone to success, not as a roadblock.

3 | Perfectionism and the fear of making mistakes can be significant obstacles to taking responsibility. It's essential to understand that there's no such thing as a perfect scenario, and any mistakes can be corrected. Even when we were in school, we were allowed to perform 'error correction.' Where did that mindset go as we grew up?

We've discovered that by not taking responsibility for ourselves, we essentially entrust our lives to others. In simpler terms, we transfer the responsibility for our own lives onto someone else. But to whom? If you have a clear vision for your future, your life, then who bears the blame if it doesn't unfold as you envisioned? Criminals who act alone often deny their guilt, yet when their actions are part of a larger protest or crowd, some proudly admit their involvement. Why is this? Because, in such cases, responsibility is distributed among several people, not just one. Shifting or sharing the blame with others is easier than accepting it entirely on your own. However, as you construct your life, it becomes imperative to learn to shoulder complete responsibility and take a stand for every thought and word.

What are the limiting thought patterns that might still be hindering your progress?

1 | Playing the victim: Holding others responsible for the current state of your life, believing that life is conspiring against you, and feeling stuck with the conviction that no one can assist you in changing your habits and life.

2 | Doubting your capabilities: Imposed or self-imposed blocks over time, negative self-talk, and anticipating future scenarios, often leaning towards negativity, leading to the belief that it's not worth starting anything at all.

3 | Misdirected energy: Engaging in unhealthy habits, succumbing to addictions, or getting distracted by activities that drain energy, creating emptiness, fatigue, powerlessness, and negative energies.

4 | Mismatched connections: Taking responsibility becomes easier when surrounded by individuals with similar goals and challenges. They don't have to be identical or in competition, but finding motivation, support, and inspiration is simpler among like-minded people.

5 | Unsuitable environment: If you think your surroundings are hindering your goals, it's essential to be honest with yourself and consider a change. Just like trying to become a skier in a warm climate or a

surfer in the mountains, achieving your ambitions might require a shift to an environment conducive to your goals.

6 | Lack of a clear goal: Assuming responsibility is challenging without a specific goal and associated tasks. If the broader picture seems daunting, break down the goal into smaller, manageable tasks, ensuring there's at least one action you can take today to move closer to your objective.

7 | External influences: Anything external that distracts your thoughts, including people, the environment, or global events. Recognize that external events may not have as much impact as they seem, and focus on the good things that you can be grateful for when going to bed.

8 | Destructive qualities: Fear, shame, skepticism, envy, and any trait where your ego looks outward instead of finding strength within. Release envy, shame, and anything holding your ego back, and shift towards a mindset that says, "I want it too!" instead of thinking someone else doesn't deserve it.

SELF-DISCIPLINE AND ITS IMPACT ON WELL-BEING

Self-discipline is the capacity to progress toward your objectives despite physical and emotional challenges. It's crucial to recognize that self-discipline is a skill only you can nurture. It is akin to habits, but unlike habits, which can be linked to negative behaviors, self-discipline involves cultivating and refining positive habits until they become second nature.

The benefits of discipline are extensive, with one of the most significant being its positive influence on self-confidence. When you adhere to disciplined practices, honoring the commitments you've made to yourself, you reinforce self-assurance. Conversely, neglecting your commitments, such as skipping workouts or consuming unhealthy food, can breed feelings of letdown and guilt. This erosion of self-trust may lead to a sense of insignificance and powerlessness, hindering your ability to fulfill promises to yourself.

In response, individuals might seek validation through excessive help for others, unintentionally punishing themselves. Rationalizing this behavior as indispensability, one may convince themselves of having unique responsibilities. However, it's crucial to recognize that no one is irreplaceable, and overburdening oneself can lead to burnout.

The key is not to view self-discipline as punitive; actions need not be driven by intense pressure. This is especially true for women, as coercion can significantly impact their well-being. For women, embracing the natural flow of creation, being, and letting go is essential. Unlike the male 'style' associated with testosterone, women don't need to force things. Recognizing hormonal differences is vital, as testosterone, responsible for motivation, goal pursuit, and competition, operates differently in men and women.

Setting goals, especially for women, should not be approached as a competitive race. Instead, it's about embracing life's journey with ease and joy, pursuing dreams without control or coercion. Easy, calm actions can replace rigid demands.

Moreover, self-discipline correlates with dopamine levels in the body. Dopamine, linked to motivation and reward, surges when pursuing goals persistently. Conversely, a low dopamine level, coupled with elevated serotonin, occurs when lethargy dominates life. This highlights the importance of maintaining a balanced lifestyle, including a proper diet, regular exercise, healthy sleep, and limited alcohol consumption.

**In essence, self-discipline is
not about rigidity but about
cultivating a mindset that effortlessly
propels you toward your aspirations,
enhancing well-being and
overall satisfaction.**

Dopamine, found in coffee, contributes to the familiar wake-up effect experienced in the morning. However, consuming coffee too early may disrupt the natural development of dopamine, leading to increased fatigue throughout the day. To optimize its benefits, it's recommended to reserve coffee for moments requiring heightened focus and improved memory during specific tasks. Conversely, individuals predisposed to anxiety or experiencing a somewhat depressed state are advised to exclude coffee from their routine, as it can further stimulate the limbic nervous system. In such cases, alternatives like cocoa or tea are recommended, topics we'll delve into in later chapters.

The term "discipline" often carries connotations of restriction, stemming from childhood experiences. It might evoke memories of stifling commands and forced actions against one's will. However, true discipline is not about external control but is a self-developed trait rooted in habits and subsequent rewards. Childhood commands, if perceived as punitive, may have shaped a negative view of discipline. It's crucial to differentiate external control from inner determination and self-discipline.

Self-discipline revolves around listening to oneself, an art that involves leading and managing one's own actions—a profound expression of self-love. It is not about coercion but a conscious alignment with personal goals. Consider the role of a coach or mentor—they guide, motivate, and, to some extent, control your actions, ensuring your focus remains on your chosen goals. Unlike your internal thoughts that may drift into laziness and negativity, a coach consistently directs your attention towards your objectives, making self-discipline more achievable. The essence of self-discipline lies in the mind and routine activities that form habits, with the outcome serving as a reward. The key is to approach every task consciously and with presence, fostering a positive connection between disciplined actions and personal fulfillment.

BRIDGE OF RESPONSIBILITY

Imagine self-discipline as a sturdy bridge connecting your aspirations with their realization. Picture this bridge spanning a vast gorge, with a tumultuous river below. Despite the challenges, crossing to the opposite bank is imperative. Envision the "old" shore as a place devoid of choices, compelling you to construct your bridge.

Divide a page into four sections and list:

1. Things accomplished today.
2. Things intended but left undone.

In the first category, note tasks initiated by your inner drive. These are actions aligned with your nature and calling—tasks you consciously or subconsciously desired to fulfill. For instance, writing a book, morning runs, a banana breakfast, or an evening sauna. Recognize these as manifestations of self-responsibility.

In the second category, document tasks you intended to do but didn't. Analyze the reasons—was it laziness, fear, or other factors? Understanding these reasons enables you to turn these aspirations into reality tomorrow.

The remaining sections involve external influences:

3. Tasks suggested by others that you executed.
4. Tasks suggested by others that you declined.

In the third category, acknowledge tasks prompted by external suggestions—actions not initially aligned with your goals. Evaluate whether these supported your calling or impeded your internal impulses. The fourth category entails tasks suggested by others that you chose not to do, prioritizing actions more crucial to you.

Examine these lists—identify the most comprehensive one. Consider the stability of this metaphorical bridge. Does it withstand the fast-flowing river of unaccomplished tasks beneath it? Assess whether the components align with your values and whether unfinished tasks are merely distractions left under the bridge.

If dissatisfied, use this awareness as a guide for improvement. Identify time-wasting activities, external influences, or excuses hindering your progress. Create this list daily, gradually refining your ability to discern what to reject and what to integrate into your routine. Over time, you'll cultivate a stable bridge, reinforcing your journey to follow your calling, elevating your confidence.

SMALL STEPS: THE KEY TO SUCCESS IN ANY GOAL

A swift journey to your goal doesn't necessitate taking giant leaps immediately. Speed isn't determined by the size of the step but by its regularity. Whether it's starting a fitness routine, adopting a healthier diet, improving your workspace, learning a new language, acquiring a skill, organizing your home, or reading a book, initiate your journey with the tiniest possible step.

For instance, embracing a healthier lifestyle might begin by opting for stairs over the elevator. If running is your goal, simply don your workout gear and step outside for a walk around the house at a set time. For healthier eating, start with a daily apple or a slice. Learning a new language can commence with mastering one word a day, repeating it whenever possible.

The brain thrives on joy, and it appreciates the avoidance of extremes. Few of us would willingly endure over a decade of high school and college again. True joy emerges when we avoid extremes, understanding that consistent effort, not one grand event, yields results. Recognizing our limits lets us relish the process, preventing the undue pressure for immediate outcomes.

The impulse to achieve goals quickly often leads to pushing beyond our capabilities, fostering negative associations. Consider the pain following intense exercise after deciding to lose all weight in a single session. Results stem from regular activities, so acknowledge that daily, even for just 15 minutes, is more valuable than occasional lengthy two-hour sessions.

Your awareness shapes the narrative. Be present when you embark on new habits—putting on running shoes, washing salad in the kitchen, or writing that first Spanish word. Presence aids your brain in understanding and internalizing positive actions, paving the way for sustained progress. Run effortlessly, make it enjoyable, and your body will yearn for it more frequently and for longer durations.

Do just enough to cultivate the desire for a little more. The gradual or "boil the frog" strategy is impactful. Gradual changes help you acclimate to new conditions, making subsequent small adjustments seem less daunting. Eventually, without realizing it, you'll find yourself at the summit of your achievement, all thanks to the power of small, consistent steps.

TIPS FOR CULTIVATING SELF-DISCIPLINE

1 | Implementing good habits: Commence by incorporating positive actions. Cultivate good habits first before contemplating relinquishing detrimental ones. Channel your energy into fostering new and better habits, and watch as the old, harmful ones naturally fade away.

2 | Establishing a routine: Abandon time constraints and devise a plan that aligns with your preferences. Minimize tasks driven by external influences and assert yourself, prioritizing your responsibilities over others'. Embrace moments of boredom, where you invent new pursuits and discover your genuine desires.

3 | Setting goals: Develop a vision and outline key objectives. Contemplate what anecdotes you'll share with guests on your 100th birthday and envision the celebration that will unfold.

4 | Reward system: Identify what propels you forward and brings you joy. Embrace the practice of rewarding yourself—it's a crucial tool for sustained motivation.

5 | Mantra: Craft a concise, positive, and potent affirmation to recite when motivation wanes. Examples include, "I'm prioritizing my health!" or "By enhancing myself, I'm positively impacting the world around me." Repeat your mantra as needed to fortify confidence and inch closer to your dreams.

The five-second rule: Confront difficulty in initiating tasks by counting backward—five, four, three, two, one. Treat it like a rocket launch—once initiated, there's no turning back. This technique triggers the brain to signal that it's time to take action. It's a proven method—try it, even for getting out of bed in the morning!

Maintaining a diary: Engage in self-reflection by documenting daily events and activities each evening. Review your accomplishments, identify preferences, and note any deviations from your plan. Regularly assess where your time is invested, empowering you to proactively thwart time-wasting activities and prioritize efforts toward your goals. Over time, this practice enhances your awareness and responsiveness to potential time thieves.

AFFIRMATIONS

Affirmations, revisited throughout this guide, are positive statements, typically framed in the first person. The mind lacks the ability to distinguish truth from falsehood, making affirmations a powerful tool to counteract negative self-talk. When incorporating new positive habits, replace self-criticism with affirmations to reshape your thoughts and instill belief in your inherent good qualities.

When practicing affirmations, sincerity is paramount. The goal is to genuinely recognize and acknowledge the positive changes within yourself. Employ affirmations after even the smallest step toward cultivating new habits. It's effortless to identify aspects of oneself that are disliked, but remember, things can always be worse. Acknowledge and appreciate your current state—recognize your goodness, beauty, and health. Life's experiences may not always emphasize these qualities, but that's precisely why self-affirmations are vital—to daily remind yourself of your inherent value, beauty, and capacity for love.

AFFIRMATIONS FOR RESPONSIBILITY AND SELF-DISCIPLINE

I willingly and joyfully take responsibility for my life.

Despite any dissatisfaction with my past, I accept it and assume responsibility for today.

I shape my tomorrow by living the today I desire.

I happily establish realistic goals and effortlessly attain them.

Daily, I prioritize what is essential to create the life I envision.

My life unfolds in alignment with my desires, or even better.

Through responsibility, I amplify my personal power.

With the growth of my discipline, my confidence soars.

Staying committed to self-discipline is simple as it propels my personal growth.

Every day, I evolve into a superior version of myself.

I willingly and joyfully take responsibility for my health, appearance, and financial well-being.

I choose to live in harmony with my values and principles.

I take responsibility for my thoughts, words, and actions, even when corrections or regrets are necessary—I am only human and embrace responsibility for all.

Self-discipline effortlessly guides me toward creating the future I envision.

***

DARE!

How often have you felt the desire to do something, say something, or go somewhere, only to find yourself hesitating or unable to act? The reasons behind this reluctance or incapacity are worth exploring. What lies at the root of not being able to follow through?

Courage is a scarce attribute in today's world. Have you ever been commended for an act that others deemed brave, yet you felt it was merely instinctual and not particularly remarkable? This is the result of acting on a calling, following an impulse without dwelling on potential outcomes, as you possessed unwavering confidence.

Ignorance, at times, works in our favor. It allows to act without the burden of foreseeing outcomes or being influenced by others' experiences. The lack of preconceived notions lets us move forward without heeding external opinions or fears. However, when we become aware of others' failures in similar pursuits, we might hesitate due to a fear of failure, even when we don't know if we are destined for the same outcome.

Failure is subjective; it depends on one's perspective. Failing to secure a job offer after ten interviews may be seen as a setback, but if the experience prepares you for a successful eleventh interview, then the initial attempts were not failures but stepping stones to eventual success. The key is in how you perceive situations and extract value from them.

Success is contingent upon preparedness to receive it. Just as children are not ready to drive a car, their brains are not developed sufficiently to multitask, predict outcomes, evaluate situations, and make informed decisions. The teenage years are crucial for brain development, particularly the frontal cortex responsible for risk-taking and decision-making. Parenting styles play a role, as overly protective parents might hinder risk-taking and decision-making development.

Brain development requires engagement and training, much like muscle growth. The age of 18, often considered the age of majority, doesn't mark a sudden transformation but is a societal benchmark based on the average rate of brain development. Brain scans can reveal the functionality of different brain parts, helping assess maturity levels and potential eligibility for punishment. Traumatic experiences in childhood or adolescence can accelerate maturity, fostering qualities like courage and decision-making skills.

Essentially, taking action requires
grasping the intricate interplay of courage,
ignorance, and how our
experiences contribute to molding
our preparedness for
confronting challenges.

Why are we delving into this topic? What does all of this have to do with courage? The truth is, courage is inherent in us from birth. As infants, we are oblivious to the complexities of the world, following our instincts fearlessly. Until someone warns us about potential dangers or suggests that our ambitious ideas are bound to fail, we don't harbor fear simply because we lack the knowledge of why we should. Sadly, our intuition and innate curiosity, which propel us forward in life, often get stifled from a very young age. Consequently, we cease engaging in intriguing and seemingly daunting pursuits, as we start believing these to be unattainable feats only for the bold. In reality, we should resist listening to others' opinions. While it may be tempting to heed advice once or twice, each time we venture forth, we confront new arguments dictating how, what, and why to do or not do. What about past memories? How do we gain the courage to follow our intuition and instincts for the rest of our lives, free from the influence of our inner voice or neighbors attempting to deter us from pursuing both small and significant aspirations?

Courage involves taking action even when the outcome is uncertain. A person might be deemed brave when parachuting for the first time, but with subsequent jumps, they simply become professionals.

As mentioned earlier, courage is inherently within us, but there is always a temptation to rationalize, saying, "I won't be able to because...", "I won't succeed because...", or "It's not for me because...". How do we respond to these nagging questions? Typically, they conceal events from the past—a confluence of circumstances that, at that specific moment, led to one outcome over another, leaving an unpleasant impression and the assumption that it's not meant for us, that it won't work. However, it's crucial to highlight the phrase "a combination of various circumstances, which at that specific moment...". These are key words that unlock your future! Past situations don't repeat themselves—they can't. Something can never unfold exactly the same way as in the past because it was a unique confluence of circumstances at that particular moment. If you don't learn from your mistakes, it's a choice, not a failure. The present is different; you're older, wiser, and countless events have occurred, creating an entirely different set of circumstances than in the past.

Hence, dwelling on the past is fruitless. Recall it only to relive the joy or excitement of certain moments, not to wallow in regrets or failures, serving as a reason to abstain from action today or hinder the planning of future goals and dreams. Realizing that the past is irrelevant, as conditions were different then and are completely distinct now, is liberating. At that moment, a newfound understanding emerges, revealing how much time has been wasted on worry, self-doubt, inaction, risk avoidance.

Yes, time may have been lost, but as we've established, everyone receives what they are prepared to accept, and everything unfolds in its own time. If you had freed yourself from doubt ten years ago, chances are you might have ventured down a different path, missing out on what you have today. However, dwelling on such possibilities is unproductive. The paramount focus is on maintaining this newfound courage. As you initiate action and make unconventional decisions, internal voices will attempt to obstruct you intermittently, and old destructive thoughts will resurface. Overcoming and disregarding them necessitates deep, likely uncomfortably deep, introspection. This process enables you to comprehend why you lack courage, and in doing so, you may embark on a journey of rewriting your life. Becoming brave entails learning to forgive, and that often requires digging deep within oneself.

FORGIVENESS

Learning to forgive is akin to presenting a gift – give what you would desire to receive, but refrain from anticipating reciprocity.

Have you ever engaged in a conflict with someone, only to reconcile through communication and forgiveness? Reflect on the instances when anger, offense, or distress gripped you – how often did you express these emotions to the other person? Not to condemn them, but to openly convey your feelings in that moment, articulating the emotions and the reasons behind your reactions.

Frequently, we cling to past words or actions, projecting them into the future, anticipating their recurrence. Our past words shape our future. Similarly, we allow our past actions to hinder present choices due to feelings of guilt or shame. What links these situations, preventing us from acting on an improved version of ourselves? The answer is straightforward – our struggle to forgive. To move forward, we must learn to forgive ourselves and others.

We often dwell on past events, feeling ashamed. What does forgiveness truly entail? How can we forgive someone unaware of causing offense? The essence of forgiveness lies in attaining inner peace and unraveling the reasons behind past occurrences. It isn't about apologies or verbal requests for forgiveness. If burdened by guilt for past actions, the person to forgive is oneself. Understand the motives behind your actions, attain peace, and ensure your present and future are not marred by painful experiences. While forgiveness is challenging to define, psychologists generally agree on a term: a conscious, deliberate decision to release negative feelings toward a person or group, regardless of whether they merit forgiveness.

<hr>

Curiosity instills the courage to explore "what ifs," while forgiveness empowers the mind to take action. The amalgamation of these two traits creates an unstoppable force.

<hr>

I'll share my personal journey, delving into the lengths I went to identify whom and how to forgive, overcoming one of my subconscious "blocks."

When I was a teenager, I occasionally had to participate in fashion shows and photo shoots. My sister was embarking on her journey as a designer, and, conveniently, I had the height that matched the parameters of a model. This allowed me to partake in various fashion shows and photo shoots, showcasing her outfits. I genuinely enjoyed the experience—although it was a bit unnerving, it was undeniably fascinating. High heels didn't bother me, and moving confidently in feminine dresses felt relatively natural. I eagerly anticipated the time when this feminine and elegant style could become my everyday attire, though I knew it wasn't quite suitable for school. As years passed, my fondness for feminine clothing persisted, and I could comfortably try them on in stores, take pictures, and so on. However, I lacked the courage to incorporate them into my daily life.

I was acutely aware that wearing such outfits would draw attention, and I feared potential comments. The thought of receiving compliments, in particular, unnerved me. Even if I opted for a less feminine look, there was always someone, often men, who, whether sitting on a sidewalk with a bottle of alcohol or walking my way, would compliment me on my appearance. I despised such comments and people in general. Due to this aversion, I tried to dress even more inconspicuously, hoping to avoid notice. Unfortunately, this tactic didn't diminish the number of compliments. My fear and distaste seemed to attract exactly what I wished to avoid.

An unfortunate incident occurred when I changed my place of residence. I moved into a building where a family lived, and there was a man who enjoyed drinking and, as I discovered, commenting on my appearance. His attempts at flattery reached a point of extreme disgust, prompting me to actively avoid him. I wouldn't greet him, pretended not to hear anything with headphones in my ears, or even avoided entering the building when he was in the yard. Unfortunately, avoidance wasn't a viable solution.

It's worth noting that I had no fear of these men molesting or harming me, as I was always prepared to defend myself with my wit. Nevertheless, I couldn't comprehend why these comments affected me so profoundly, rendering me powerless against mere words.

However, I was deeply disturbed by those drunken looks and attempts at flattery. It prompted me to delve into why I had this aversion to this type of man, why I was so concerned about being noticed, why I didn't want to be complimented (how is it possible that a woman doesn't want to be complimented?), why I couldn't go out in society dressed femininely, as I always wanted, and why I avoided being respected. How could men treat a woman like that? And then, click! This question was the key to everything! Suddenly, everything fell into place, and answers to many questions were found. Now the most unpleasant part of this story will begin, but I will try to convey it as delicately as possible, so that you can comprehend how "deep" you have to dig within yourself.

When I was 19, I moved to Denmark. I shared an apartment with a Latvian guy who was around 30 at the time. Accommodation in Denmark is quite expensive, especially for foreign students, and finding a place is challenging. You have to endure long lines for dormitories, so living with this man seemed like a practical solution. Besides, he was an acquaintance of a girl I knew who had also lived in Denmark for many years. Living with someone familiar felt safer than with a complete stranger or alone. This was my perception - it felt safer not to be alone, especially since I returned home from work on night shifts very late (around 5 in the morning). If I had technical issues, he was always available to help. I should add that he sometimes had a beer in the evenings, and occasionally a friend would join him. It didn't bother me, and I never felt concerned about inappropriate behavior. The only annoyance was the lingering smell of alcohol in the kitchen in the morning, which could have been easily remedied by airing it out.

One Friday night, I returned home a bit earlier than usual, around three o'clock. As I entered the apartment, I headed straight to the kitchen, located directly opposite the front door. I heard sounds and realized he was not alone. I understood - okay, I've interrupted my solitude, which is understandable, as I came home earlier than expected! I stepped outside for a moment to contemplate my options and decided that despite the discomfort, it was my apartment too. Exhausted and with a night shift the next day, I needed sleep. I reasoned that I could drown out the noises with loud music through my headphones and quickly fall asleep. In the morning, I would avoid eye contact to minimize awkwardness, and when the opportunity arose, I would communicate my preferences to avoid similar situations in the future. With this plan in mind, I went upstairs and proceeded directly to my room through the long corridor, passing his door, trying to ignore the sounds. It's important to note that our rooms shared a wall, making it nearly impossible not to hear the sounds.

Upon entering my room, I immediately recognized a voice that wasn't my roommate's. My internal feelings shifted - no longer discomfort about entering my apartment but curiosity, accompanied by wariness. Who was in my flat?! Feeling a bit threatened, I opted not to put on my headphones and instead waited to observe the situation. The voices of women grew louder, and the man's voice spoke again. It became evident that it was not my roommate. I speculated that he had assisted a friend by lending keys for a place to stay after a party. It was an impractical notion, but given the central location and cold weather, somewhat understandable. However, I decided not to let this situation occur again. As the sounds intensified and persisted for an uncomfortably long time, my fear materialized - I heard my roommate's voice in the room. There were three of them, just having a good time. Oh, how repulsive it began to seem to me! This is my home, too! The voices grew unbearably loud. The woman's voice no longer conveyed pleasure and happiness; it sounded more like screams. I contemplated making a loud noise to make them stop, as I felt intensely uncomfortable, a bit scared, and, most importantly, I wanted to alleviate the woman's apparent distress.

Suddenly, the loud screams ceased, leaving only the men's voices and conversations audible. Although I couldn't discern their words, I just wanted to escape the situation, not to sleep all night but to vacate these rooms. However, as I attempted to leave my room, my roommate and his friend emerged from the adjacent room, both naked. Both were holding the unconscious woman by her arms and legs, also naked. Terrified, I hastily retreated into my room, as I certainly didn't want to get close to them. With the front door facing the bathroom, leaving was no longer an option.

I barricaded the door with a chest of drawers, just in case. However, deep down, I knew I wasn't in immediate danger. I felt a sense of assurance, not that I was certain about confronting them aggressively out of anger, hitting them with something heavy, etc. However, all I did was attempt to peer through the keyhole in the dark to discern what was transpiring at the end of the corridor and ascertain whether the woman had lost consciousness or... Fortunately, she had only passed out. In the bathroom, they assisted her in vomiting, but what unfolded afterward was appalling. One of them had returned to the room, while the other, emerging from the bathroom, held her by the arms, dragging her feet on the floor, and pulled the woman back into the room. It was repulsive, profoundly repulsive. But, at least, it seemed to be over. Or so I thought. Regrettably, I was mistaken because a moment later, the sounds resumed. Without hesitation, I decided not to stay in the apartment. Hastily, I gathered my essential belongings and left my room.

As I passed by, I saw an even more disturbing scene because his door had not been closed. It was utterly revolting. After exiting, I was unsure about what to do next. Should I call the police? What should I tell them? Do I even officially reside here? What is the phone number for the police? How do you pronounce the name of this street? What the hell am I supposed to do, it's already four in the morning!!! I phoned my best Latvian friend, also residing in Copenhagen, hoping that he was either working a night shift or still awake due to a party—either scenario would work for me. Thankfully, he was available. I briefed him on the approximate situation, and he graciously offered me refuge. I had to take the expensive subway for a few stops, but there were no other options. While relieved to be safe, I cried over what I had witnessed. Despite the emotional turmoil, it wasn't difficult to fall asleep.

The next day, my work began at 17:00. By then, I had managed to clean up and compose myself to go to the restaurant where I work as a bartender. Around 3:00 PM, when I had to return to my apartment to collect my belongings, I found myself oscillating between anger and calmness, contemplating everything that transpired the previous night and what I would say to my flatmate, what ultimatum I would present, etc. Upon opening the apartment door, my roommate emerged directly from the toilet, still naked, and sounds still emanated from the room—everything was still happening!!! In shock and disgust, when he noticed me, he casually said, "Ugh, bye!" I promptly slammed the door shut and headed straight for my workplace. Reflecting on this distressing incident, answers to all my questions became clear—this is why I despise the alcohol-clouded gazes of men, their audacity to offer compliments—they scrutinized my height. By what right?!

How can someone treat a woman so disrespectfully? It was evident that this was a disdain for men who do not respect a woman and her body, and it took about 10 years for me to realize that the seemingly forgotten event of that night had still left a mark on me. I forgave them. I didn't make excuses, but my flatmate later told me apologetically that they had taken some kind of pill, unaware of its consequences. While ignorance doesn't excuse responsibility, their brains weren't functioning properly at the time. The loudest assurance I heard was the promise that nothing like that would ever happen again. In any case, I had forgiven and healed my trauma.

Afterward, I became brave. I no longer avoided men of this type; on the contrary, I began to test whether I had overcome this "block." To my surprise, my downstairs neighbor stopped saying "Hi!" (usually followed by a compliment) and instead started saying a simple "Hello!" Another significant incident occurred when, while walking in a rather remote place, three drunk men and one woman approached me. I considered turning back, but there was nowhere to disappear. I thought, "No, I'll just pass them. They're only people, anything can happen, I'll just pass them, maybe even look someone in the eye." Unexpectedly, one of the drunken men said to me, "Hello!" The other immediately joined in, teasing him with,

"Stop, don't do that!" It was unexpected! One of the group addressed me, and the other defended me. And I knew—yes, I got rid of this! Finally! I must say that such situations have not occurred to me since, at least not that I can remember.

However, one thing persisted—I still couldn't dress in a feminine way, with a plunging neckline or high heels. Was it related? It turns out, yes. I hadn't forgiven myself yet. I really didn't know what to do in that situation; every option had its pros and cons, and in the end, I did absolutely nothing! Not because I didn't want to, but because I logically decided that the best course of action was to protect myself and walk away from that situation. What prevented me from forgiving myself was the uncertainty about the best course of action. Did she do it willingly? Was she paid for it? Was it her routine? Did she remember it? Did she even survive? I do not know. Some might say the police should have been called, others that I did the right thing by running away, and still others that I should have intervened. I agree with everyone, but I am well aware that there was no right or wrong in that situation. I can't fix every mistake someone else has made. All I can do is take care of myself, take responsibility for myself, think positive thoughts, whatever keeps me safe day and night, and hope that no one ever ends up in my role or that woman's role.

Each person has their own story, reasons, and path to follow. Everyone makes mistakes and learns from them. I have no right to judge the mistakes of others; I am not responsible for the lessons everyone has to go through. I didn't share this disgusting incident with anyone for ten years until finally, by talking to myself and voicing it to someone else, I forgave all the drunken men in the world and myself. Now, I can dress boldly (which I consider simply feminine) and showcase my beautiful body (within the limits of the norm), as our bodies are truly beautiful. Though it's not easy to share this story, I try to see it as a failed film whose director didn't really know what he was doing. I no longer associate this experience with myself; it could have been anyone else in my place.

Discussing this trauma here is quite brave because I expose myself to judgment, but I don't care because I have forgiven myself for my actions at the time and know that it was the best thing I could have done then. I hope that you, too, will resolve some deep-seated, perhaps forgotten pain or trauma that prevents you from realizing your dreams. Even though forgiveness is not always easy, know that it is necessary and worth every tear shed to live with ease in the future. Do not leave the energy in the hands of those who hurt your mind; forgive yourself and others. Be brave so that you can enjoy each day exactly as you want.

Learn to forgive anyone who has hurt you. Yes, it happened to you, but instead of you, it could have been anyone else. Don't let this incident define you, no matter how difficult it may be. By "dumping" their problems, the abuser hurts you. Yes, it wasn't right, but it doesn't have to be a reason for you to limit your future because of it. Forgive, and you will open the door to freedom much wider.

A COURAGE TO BE VULNERABLE

Let me clarify what I mean by the word "weak." By it, I intend to encompass qualities such as trust, openness, love, generosity, and the ability to forgive. These are the attributes a person must possess to choose not to engage in conflict but to simply live in peace.

In my early 20s, I attended a company Christmas party with a guy I was dating at the time. The event was splendid, the venue exquisitely decorated, and over 100 elegantly dressed guests enjoyed fine food and drinks, including me in my newly bought elegant dress. As the evening progressed into a more relaxed atmosphere with dancing, I decided to leave the dance floor and approach one of the "main" tables where the most prominent people were seated.

Approaching the table and beginning to sit on the chosen chair turned out to be the longest moment of my life. In a fraction of a second, I realized that the chair was no longer there, and I found myself falling face down onto the floor in my new dress and flimsy pantyhose. Ouch! Physically hurt? Yes. Emotionally hurt? Absolutely! To add to the sting, I saw a big, wide smile on the face of my boyfriend at the time, who was now laughing heartily. It was a moment of humiliation.

Feeling humiliated and hurt, I faced a revelation. The person I thought cared about me chose to mock and hurt me in front of everyone. How "manly" and respectful! Despite the alcohol involved, it was certainly no excuse. How did I react? I chose not to argue, not to fight, and not to humiliate him in return. Instead, I swallowed the pain, vowing never to be weak again.

This experience led me to harden myself, to strive for strength and improvement at the cost of losing my true self. However, this didn't bring the desired results. Comments like 'you're not feminine', 'you're acting like a psychopath', 'stop exaggerating' followed. I had allowed the empty words and foolish actions of another to influence me, suppressing my emotions and feelings.

Eventually, I realized the importance of not suppressing emotions and allowing myself to be vulnerable. It's a lesson learned early, and now, in my prime, I understand the value of opening up. I am still learning to be "weak" and embrace emotions and feelings. It is essential to acknowledge that events in the past may make it scary to expose oneself again, but it's crucial for personal growth. Dear ladies, understand that a man's behavior, especially public embarrassment, is often a reflection of his own wounded "inner child" or damaged male ego from previous experiences, not a judgment of your worth.

If a man cannot take pride in his woman, it reflects his insecurity about himself. Similarly, men, the same principle applies in the opposite direction. In reality, the experience of being "weak" (loving, faithful, forgiving) can be most beautiful when you are with the right person. If you find it challenging to express your emotions and true feelings, it may indicate that you haven't yet found your right place. To discover it, you must be courageous enough to embrace vulnerability. This journey can transform into a beautiful experience, affirming that everything is unfolding as it should.

People should not enter new relationships with a hardened heart just because someone in the past failed to appreciate their positive qualities. Humans are designed to love and be loved, not to conceal their true selves by becoming emotionally guarded, or to be stingy in giving because of past betrayals. Regardless of what the past holds, strive to rediscover your capacity for vulnerability—to give and receive freely—and embrace the freedom you were genuinely created to experience.

We were born brave.
We only grew up to be afraid.

HOW TO UNDERSTAND WHAT IS
STOPPING YOUR COURAGE

When you harbor an idea, a desire, a dream, or a goal to initiate something, but it remains stagnant without further action, take a moment to introspect. Ask yourself questions to unravel the reasons behind your hesitation. Is it not your priority at the moment? Are you lacking necessary resources or competence to take action? Recognize that these factors can be changed and adjusted to manifest your aspirations. Envision creating conditions that enable the realization of your idea. What thoughts are dominating your mind? Can you visualize your dream and picture yourself in the "what if" scenario?

The emergence of an idea is a signal that you have the capability to bring it to fruition. If you can visualize and imagine specific situations, you are subconsciously prepared for them. Whether it's material, spiritual, or health-related aspirations, do not suppress these thoughts with self-condemnation. Write down every idea that comes to you—they are guiding signs toward something meant for you. Take that initial step immediately, embracing the concept of "momentum"—catching a thought and translating it into prompt action. In those moments, you connect with your intuition, higher self, or the universe, signifying that your subconscious holds insights capable of transforming your life. Act promptly and without excuses, showing readiness to receive your dreams.

How to act to avoid hindering your own bravery:

1 | Don't predict the future - Resist the urge to keep things quiet, phrase words differently, or avoid situations based on negative projections of the future. Challenge thoughts like "it won't work out" or "they won't agree." Realize that predicting future scenarios negatively, based on past experiences, is irrational. Since the past no longer exists, envision positive scenarios, elevate your vibrations, and attract miracles into your life by boldly acting towards your goals.

2 | Ask yourself questions and overcome limits - challenge yourself with introspective questions. Identify your desires and ponder on what holds you back. If, for instance, you wish to pursue music but feel incapable, ask why. Question the negative beliefs like "I can't do music." Analyze the origin of such beliefs—is it a lingering influence from the past, perhaps a second-grade teacher's criticism? Remember, the past is non-existent. Skills, including musicality, can be developed. Forgive past judgments, whether self-inflicted or from others, and recognize that maturity and preferences evolve over time. It's never too late to embark on a new path.

3 | Forgive in thoughts - forgiveness need not involve informing the person. The act is for your peace, not theirs. People may unintentionally cause harm, or misunderstandings may occur. Focus on how it affected you and the lesson it imparted. Reflect on your future actions, acknowledging the potential impact of your words or actions on others.

4| Embrace trials with joy - identify triggers and welcome challenges with joy. Recognize repeated trials as opportunities for growth. Use these instances to reshape your perspective, attitude, and actions. Over time, triggers may lose their power, or you may respond differently.

5| Approach it as a game - visualize the healing process as a game with multiple levels. If you stumble at a level, restart with newfound courage. Each level presents opportunities for transformation. Embrace the journey, knowing that as you progress, challenges become stepping stones. Laugh at your past apprehensions and be prepared to view your current state with the same perspective in the future. Start boldly, knowing that each step contributes to your personal growth.

HOW TO BECOME BRAVE

This is a broad concept, but the best feeling you'll experience is when what you once considered bravery becomes your new normal. Recognize that pursuing your dream or goal is not an act of bravery; it's merely moving toward what you desire, and this should be your new normal!

Is there a singular way to forgive and be brave? For me, it's associated with open conversations with myself, expressing pain and resentment out loud, even if tears fall. You must acknowledge your guilt or any painful aspects and accept that the past is behind you, and that's a good thing. Sometimes, being aware of this problem is the key to freeing yourself, but at times, you might need to undergo a "deep cleaning" over several years. Either way, the result is worth it.

There is no distinction between big or small courage; it simply exists or doesn't.

What does healing mean? How can you ensure you are healed, and how can you make it easier and less painful? Healing is not a difficult and painful process unless, from the outset, you recognize that everything has changed since then and is only getting better. Position yourself to think solely about yourself and your healing from the start. Always remember, courage is within you from birth; it was just suppressed. Listen to your intuition, your inner voice, and do things that you're a little afraid of, simply because you feel you have to. Play! You can't go wrong because it's a game where you learn every step of the way, getting what you're meant to get when you're ready for it.

When you have forgiven yourself and others, you'll feel immense relief. Realizing that a weight you've been carrying, often without realizing its impact, has been lifted will instill positive confidence. Purposeful confidence doesn't mean conceited self-confidence but the awareness that you have the freedom to think and act according to your convictions. Before, if you felt strange obstacles and constant reservations impeding your way, hindering your progress, now you're aware that everything is happening as it should, and you can approach your goals with confidence. It's crucial to understand that confidence without clarity can be destructive. Therefore, first, be aware of what you want to achieve, and only then be confident in yourself, not the other way around. This sequence is vital. That's why I emphasized "targeted confidence" earlier, as it only develops when you know your destination. If you're simply self-confident, you can be easily influenced, manipulated, and pushed in directions you don't genuinely want to go. First, know what you want, understand what's preventing you, grasp why these thoughts arose, forgive, heal yourself, and gain targeted confidence, enabling you to achieve your goals.

Don't be afraid to be different, but fear not fulfilling your dreams! Taking the initiative can sometimes feel intimidating. However, if you have an idea and believe it must be implemented, don't exhaust yourself searching for followers; just start doing it. The pursuit of companions often leads to the alteration of your dream. You know the saying - as many people, so many opinions? Precisely! It's an eternal truth, and, to be honest, accepting it has been challenging for me at times, contributing to my burnout experiences.

Once upon a time, when I worked in marketing, I took every product very personally. Many times I witnessed the development of globally recognized companies, setting internal goals and creating strategies to gradually expand them, perceiving their potential. However, I often encountered obstacles when my plans lacked support. Fortunately, 95% of the products I marketed were of quality, and I genuinely wanted to introduce them to the world. I didn't need to resort to manipulation to "sell" the product; my approach was to properly showcase a great product, believing that those who appreciate it will buy it without deception. Nevertheless, my wings were often clipped; in reality, it looked like this - brimming with inspiration, I'd share my ideas, present visual solutions, outline future scenarios, only to receive a "no." And the cycle would start anew. While I could handle rejection and was understanding, maintaining inspiration in the face of self-imposed obstacles was tough. Such situations should be accepted, but adhering to something you disagree with is quite challenging, especially for a creative person. This experience inspired me to write a book about marketing and how easy it is to sell a good product if you believe in it.

Then I realized, with all these clients, it wasn't about their product; it was about them. People's personal lack of confidence, self-imposed limitations, and limiting beliefs - personal fears often hindered business growth. There was no connection between my ideas and the quality product. Once I grasped this, I understood it wouldn't be a book about marketing. I had attracted people unsure of themselves because I lacked confidence in myself. I built more and more barriers in my work, with each new client or job lowering my confidence and forcing me to think "small" to avoid feeling suffocated. Insecurity grew within me, and I began questioning myself more. However, thinking small has always bored me. There came a moment when I realized I was acting against my beliefs and intuition. It was a classic burnout scenario - the more I sought confidence, the more I invested my ideas in someone else's product. The more I faced rejection, the more my self-confidence dwindled, and my desire to create began to fade. I sought new avenues to share my ideas, only to face reprimands again. That's when I started healing myself because I knew I was not made for something simple.

When I realized that my fear of doing things differently and writing a book was rooted in the fact that my ideas had previously been labeled as "unrealistic", "impossible", "preferable", and so on, I found solace in the idea that I could create the book as if it were for myself. I could write in the way I desired, as voluminous as I wished, infusing as much of myself as I wanted. Gradually, as the desire to create returned, I developed a purposeful belief that it would surely be useful to at least one more person. I just knew it.

Then I understood that to reach this one "real" person, I needed to publish it to a broader audience and in different languages! I cultivated a purposeful belief that there was a person somewhere for whom at least one sentence here mattered, and it was my responsibility to provide them with that information. No one else would influence what thoughts I write here, what the cover design would look like, or how many languages I would translate it into. This is a healthy belief, not vanity but confidence. I am intrigued to see where this will take my book! That's how I became brave and forgave those who, in the past, made me doubt myself and evaluated my performance through their ego. It's a great feeling to know your goal, to be confident in your actions, and to enjoy the process. Are you ready to achieve your dream?

THE WHEEL OF COURAGE

Now, be completely honest with yourself. What is it that you want? Everything starts with a dream. If it is not implemented, then there is obviously something wrong with it. What is the cause of the disturbance? Forgive whoever caused it and heal! This is how you will gain confidence and be able to devote yourself to your dream.

Observe this sequence! For better understanding, take a look at the "Wheel of Courage." Another crucial aspect of the "Wheel of Courage" is to watch the opposite section of each segment! This is essential because your dream will help you forgive - it will serve as motivation. A distraction will aid in healing yourself - it will act as a tool or a challenge to improve yourself in some way. Moreover, to gain confidence, the cause will assist you because after healing, you will consider it an experience, having become more knowledgeable.

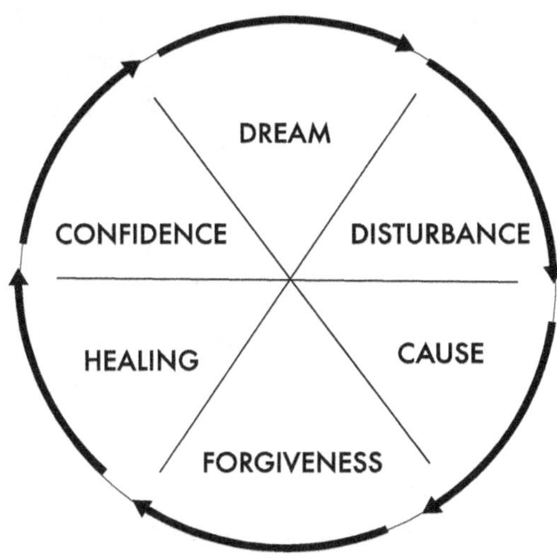

WHAT ELSE YOU NEED TO KNOW BEFORE
YOU FORGIVE

DECISION

As soon as you have identified the reason for your insecurity or past trauma, forgive immediately. Will you say that it is impossible? Think again. You just have to want it. You simply have to make that decision. By continually revisiting the past and intertwining it with your present life, you allow external forces to control you, relinquishing control of your own life. Is that what you want? Do you realize that if you desire "freedom," you won't attain it by dwelling on the past? We expend so much energy worrying about events, big and small, from the past. This can significantly impact our health. When you recall an event that caused you unpleasant emotions in the past, your body reacts as if it were happening in the present, cultivating stress, anger, shame, and other destructive emotions that exhaust your body. Your energy centers become increasingly blocked as you activate "survival" mode due to stress. Remember, with the first centers blocked, a person may feel empty, insufficient, unfulfilled, too dependent on material things and various pleasures. Not an ideal foundation for creating, loving, and giving, is it? Therefore, make the decision to stop associating yourself with the heavy events of the past. Yes, it may mean forgetting someone, perhaps someone who was once very close and dear. But remember this - you only need to forget the painful events of the past. You can always cherish the love and bright moments associated with that person. Eventually, you will also attract new, even more beautiful moments.

ADMIT YOUR MISTAKES

What could be simpler and yet more complicated than admitting your mistakes? It is entirely your choice - to continue giving your energy to the past or to admit, in a single moment, "Yes, I was wrong!" and magically free yourself from the burden, moving forward and focusing on new, positive things. Everyone makes mistakes! Don't waste energy trying to prove otherwise! You'll need that energy to create positive events!

ELIMINATING THE SENSE OF GUILT

Guilt arises when we realize that, in reality, we should have acted differently because our actions did not align with our nature. If we feel guilty for what we have done, it means our actions are not in harmony with our identity. However, that doesn't mean you should punish yourself or carry guilt. Realize that we do the best we can in every situation. If you ever feel guilty, identify the circumstances that led you to act that way and figure out how you will act differently if a similar situation arises again. The feeling of guilt arises because you acknowledge that you could have done better, but at that moment, you didn't know exactly how. Making a mistake is human, but not changing your behavior the next time is a choice.

1| White page - Most likely, while reading this section, you have already had an idea about some unresolved situation that requires forgiveness. Take a blank page and write everything that comes to mind. What happened, what was painful, how you felt then, how you feel now. Write a reply letter on the other page. If you want to forgive yourself, then write it from yourself. However, if someone else was involved, write the letter as you would like to receive it from that person. For example, "I did not know that my actions would hurt you so much. I acted like that because I was not taught otherwise. I am also human and make mistakes..." Put these two letters together and burn them. Everything! Well, this has been said and left in the past. This conversation is over, and the situation is resolved. Forget it.

2| Self-observation - Getting to know yourself is not always a pleasant process. By illuminating our dark sides, we may start to like ourselves a little less. But this is very valuable and necessary because only by being aware of our dark sides can we know what to get rid of. Start observing yourself in different situations. How do you react in situations of stress and shock? Are you quick to anger and aggression? Maybe you experience diarrhea or nausea? Perhaps palpitations start, and you suddenly want to take more control of the situation, or you start recklessly saying things you don't really mean? Everything contrary to your everyday state indicates that one of the energy centers is either under- or overactive. Even if you do not initially connect it with an event from your past, be aware that energy center blockages can occur already in the mother's body. The fetus feels and survives its world largely through the mother. Therefore, it makes a difference whether the mother lives in a constant state of stress or provides the body with joy, creating pleasant vibrations and security in which the child will be able to fully utilize the potential for happiness and creativity. The influence of parents on the child's energy, of course, continues even as they grow up. If a child whose personality is beginning to awaken does not feel loved and accepted, the solar plexus center is blocked. Although unconsciously, parents may want to bring up the child by imposing their will, leading to a constant struggle between the parents and the child. As the solar plexus center is blocked, in adulthood, they may feel a lack of courage and fear living their own life and being an individual.

Meditation - This is undoubtedly the most effective practice that every person should include in their routine, not only to remove blockages of energy centers but simply to include in everyday life, much like brushing teeth. The purpose of meditation is to get to know your thoughts, actions, and emotions by actions, and emotions by turning off the analytical mind and accessing the subconscious, where all the answers are found. Even 15 minutes a day of meditation to get to know yourself can significantly change not only your day but life in general! Meditation helps you understand yourself better. It can be done sitting, standing, lying down, or even walking! Walking meditation is said to be the most effective. For example, meditating in a sitting position may make you feel more alive, awake, and with a vision of how to act. However, after getting into the rhythm of the day, you can easily fall back into old subconscious programs. Therefore, practicing walking meditation is the most effective way to rewrite your subconscious programs permanently. About meditations, I can't provide all the information because I believe everyone has to find the way that suits them best. But even if you simply sit in a chair, close your eyes, and sit for 5 minutes, it will be a great start to see how difficult it is to sit still and observe all the thoughts going through your head! When you meditate on specific energy centers, you may feel powerless or some other unpleasant feeling. It was very pronounced for me with the first center - initially, my head was spinning, I felt nauseous, and it seemed that I was doing something wrong. But that just means that everything is right. By starting to cleanse in this way, the pent-up energy is released, and the content reappears in our consciousness. We can re-experience the same feelings - fear, anger, pain. Therefore, many people lack the courage to undertake these cleansing processes. But believe me - the feeling of ease and freedom you will get afterward will be worth it. I recommend checking out YouTube, where there is a very wide selection of guided meditations. Find your favorite teacher and get your energy moving! Then, if you want to manifest something in your life, a very popular concept today, you must first have completely organized energy. Any blockage will not allow you to get what you want because, quite simply, your vibrations do not match your dream! Free yourself, and you will get what you want.

AFFIRMATIONS FOR COURAGE AND FORGIVENESS

I forgive myself for all my mistakes and allow myself to learn
from them to become a better person every day.

I forgive others for their actions that have somehow offended
me because everyone has the right to do what they think is the
best way.

By forgiving myself and starting to love myself, others love
me too.

I easily find the cause of my fear. I easily worked out this past
situation so that it would stop affecting my future life.

I like to fill my life with bold actions and decisions.

I am a good person who deserves to forgive myself and others
and create a beautiful today and tomorrow.

Every day is filled with new opportunities.

The past is an illusion. What happened in it is gone.

All that is real is the present.

I forget people from the past and focus on people in the
present.

I forgive everyone who has ever hurt me. I send them loving and bright energy and clear my energy field from them.

I did the best I could, and that taught me how to do it next time.

I let go of all the negative emotions that have been holding me back from living the life I want.

I am valuable because of who I am.

BALANCE!

Do you have the ability to coexist and sympathize with those around you? In other words, are you an empathetic person capable of overcoming your egocentrism and putting yourself in another person's shoes to better understand their motives and feelings?

Some people lack empathy and may never develop it unless they work hard on themselves. These individuals are often referred to as narcissists. Scientists and psychologists are still studying this type of personality, and current knowledge suggests it's essentially a brain disorder—narcissists' brains don't function normally. They perceive everything through their personal prism, and their ability to empathize is limited. Narcissists are mostly shaped in childhood due to the parenting style, which plays a crucial role in brain development. Paradoxically, empathy also begins to develop in childhood, starting from preschool age, thanks to a nurturing parenting style.

A beneficial parenting style involves solving progressively more complex tasks together with adults and peers in a loving atmosphere, promoting age-appropriate interaction. Unlike the concept of forced ability development, a favorable parenting style focuses on enriching existing skills rather than accelerating them. Accelerating a child's abilities artificially may deprive them of essential childhood experiences when other critical skills are being developed. Adults should gradually involve the child in new activities that expand their social skills and enrich their inner world.

A favorable parenting style maximizes a child's talents in a safe and healthy environment, ensuring their development. If someone hasn't received a favorable parenting style but perhaps a narcissistic one, lacking empathy is a potential outcome. Lack of empathy can manifest in expecting too much from others, being easily offended, wanting things to go their way without expressing their wishes explicitly, and even manipulating situations to make others feel at fault.

Whether dealing with an insecure person or a narcissist, don't try to teach them empathy or blame them for their lack of understanding. Instead, focus on yourself and balance empathy within. It can be developed without necessarily solving others' problems or becoming overly emotional. Empathy aids in understanding different life situations, accepting the truth more easily, and navigating unwanted situations more painlessly. Balancing empathy involves evaluating each situation and adapting your actions accordingly for the best outcome.

____

Empathy is a powerful
but often invisible quality.
It enhances your ability to
analyze situations, understand others,
improve your well-being, reduce
disappointment, and react more productively.

So, how can you truly develop empathy?
It all starts with how you
perceive things.

____

WHAT IS BALANCED EMPATHY

Have you ever received poor service in a shop, cafe, or restaurant? Perhaps you asked for salt or something similar, only to receive a judgmental look, attitude, or an answer that left you wondering what you had done wrong. Did you notice that all the tables in the restaurant were occupied, and one of them had a large group of friends celebrating late into the evening, close to closing time? Now, put yourself in the shoes of the waiter. What if their new shoes were still uncomfortable, and they wanted to minimize unnecessary walking? What if they had to rush home for a child's birthday? What if they initially took the salt away to free up space on the table and then realized it was a mistake? There are numerous reasons someone might react negatively to your question, but the true reasons often accumulate throughout the day, not because of your inquiry. If you've worked as a waiter, you'll understand this perspective. Even when you strive to maintain a smile and kindness, certain circumstances can erode that positivity, especially when patience wears thin.

Consider another scenario. Your boss is a perpetual source of annoyance. Regardless of your efforts, he is never satisfied, always finding fault. Have you been in this situation? Now, look at it from your boss's perspective. He has a family, three kids, a substantial house to support, management responsibilities, and sales targets to meet—all of which contribute to his stress. You, as his assistant, may expect praise for your work, but he's under so much pressure that he vents his frustration on you. Have you ever been in a leadership position, responsible for immediate salary payments and bills, feeling like everything is the employees' fault? Childhood echoes of parents emphasizing the need to study harder and work diligently may still resonate. How can such a boss be kind and considerate to employees with these stressors? While it's ideal for everyone to hold their positions based on both professional and personal skills, this doesn't always happen. Sometimes individuals with similar qualifications to the lowest-ranking employees end up in higher positions due to their "firmness of character," causing headaches for subordinates. Nonetheless, every boss is just an ordinary person beneath the managerial role.

Leaders who passionately pursue their ideas and can distinguish between the roles of boss and subordinate, motivating employees with inspiration, are more effective than those plagued by stress and egocentrism. However, if you've encountered an unpleasant boss, remember to try to empathize by putting yourself in their shoes. It's not about doing more; it's about recognizing that they have other concerns to handle. When discussing empathy, we can understand and justify others' actions sometimes, and other times we can't. Why? Because we may not have been in the same or a similar situation. Empathy expands our perception, allowing us to understand how someone feels based on our experiences in similar situations. Empathy isn't always about justifying actions; it's about understanding the broader context and the challenges others face.

Empathy comes from broadening your perception.Perception is precisely what we mean by it - all five senses, or what we take into the body with our sense organs. Perception is the way you look at the world, things, people, and situations. The more developed your perception is, the more diverse sensations your body can feel. It is the ability to recall past or anticipate future emotions. It is an emotional experience of the body that will help you balance empathy and better understand the actions of the other person, as you will be able to empathize with their situation more easily.

If we haven't balanced our empathy, we rely solely on reason. When we hear what the other person said, for example, something that hurts or offends us, we will "let" it pass through our mind and associate it with some old program of our subconscious. In this way, we will not hear what the other person is saying but will connect it to our past, even though this person was not involved in it at all.

Taking everything only with the mind (hearing only the words and not what the other person really means) can lead people to overreact and speak before they really think. Therefore, in any conversation, there is an opportunity to ask questions, thereby clarifying the circumstances. Clarifying the circumstances gives your mind time to calm down and your body to activate the most important senses at the given moment—for example, listening to the timbre of the other person's voice with your hearing, observing his body movements with your eyes, and determining by touch how excited his heart rhythm is (if it is a very close person) and the like.

By clarifying the situation, I mean asking counter-questions rather than reacting sharply to whatever was just said that offended you. You always have the choice to ask "How did you think that?", "What prompted you to act like that?", "What is the reason for your accusations about...". The situations are so different that I will not mention more examples this time because surely each of us can imagine a situation now when perhaps we should have clarified more circumstances before we started to react sharply without thinking.

If I think about it now, would the conversation have changed if I had clarified all the circumstances? Maybe the partner's reproaches are related to his fear of the past? Perhaps the boss's anger is related to the high demands from management combined with his low self-esteem? Of course, you will not always understand the situation delicately, down to the last detail. However, by clarifying some circumstances, you can relieve yourself of the headache, realizing that the reprehensible behavior of another person is not actually related to you. By balancing empathy, you will realize that people often speak through their doubts and fears. They are operating from their own subconscious programs, but if you can sense this person's fear or insecurity and understand that all they want is not to belittle you but to gain their confidence, then you will be able to keep not only your peace, but possibly you will help the other person to overcome his "old" thinking.

Let me tell you how I learned the importance of empathy. In general, I have been quite empathic since childhood. I have always had the feeling that I want to help others, inspire and instill a sense of security in people. I easily feel the fear, insecurity, and worthlessness of others and am happy to help reduce it, if there is such an opportunity, to maximally create a feeling of equality between people and the awareness that everyone is valuable as they are. But there is an event that I still remember today and which serves as a reminder to me - before speaking, always (always!) clarify all the circumstances!

In my early youth, I was quite reserved, but I could open up with my closest friends. Mostly, I was fascinated (and nothing has changed now) by good humor. With resourceful thinking, combined with my own, I can often throw out a joke that, when shared with the interlocutor, leads to pleasant stomach cramps and laughter to tears. I was (and still am) very polite. Laughing at others or gossiping or belittling someone is not my style because I am aware that everyone has their own motivations.

So, on a hot summer day during the school holidays, my friends and I were in the center having fun. We laughed so hard that whatever everyone said next seemed even funnier than the last. It's laughing when you can't see anything around you, and all your problems are forgotten. Laughing, I heard a group of strange children a little further away calling their friend: "Come on!" Hearing this, I joined in the jokes of the company of my friends, saying: "Well, go!" And we continued to laugh. It seems, nothing crazy. And then I turned my head to see who these youths were and saw that the fellow they called had trouble with both his legs, and was limping severely, to say the least. Moving forward, but hurrying definitely didn't change his walking speed. And that one stupid comment of mine (they didn't even hear it, but it would have been enough if I had said it in my mind) made me understand - don't talk if you don't know! Don't judge if you haven't found out the facts! Do not think before you are convinced of the truth! Mostly, we never know the truth. We don't know what has happened in the other person's life, what he has felt, in what ways he has been hurt, what foreign programs he has accepted, but we allow ourselves to judge only what we can see. This is very wrong. That's why -

don't speak if you don't know! And if you say something that has angered or offended the other, then drop your "ego," clarify the circumstances and, if necessary, apologize! Eliminate the possibility that in the future you might feel guilty about this seemingly innocent comment, immediately saying: "I'm sorry if I said something offensive, I was thinking..." And that's it! People get sad, offended, and upset because an event that caused unpleasant emotions is recalled in their mind. Therefore, if you said something offensive, then apologize, but in general - first clarify the facts and only then speak.

We must learn to accept. In other words, we have to learn to accept. As soon as the line from "must learn" to "must learn" is crossed, it opens up a lot of new possibilities. If we are able to properly hold this feeling, then nothing can worry us anymore because we can look at any situation from different sides. Everything that makes us mad, we have to learn to accept without anger and understand that it is not worth worrying about. It is worth developing yourself, and it is important to appreciate it. There are things that drive us all crazy. Why? And why is it something different for everyone? What drives or triggers are things that cause certain emotions in us that we have felt in the past and that have come from negative experiences. However, if we are able to look at these "triggers" (things that irritate, make us angry) from a different angle - with a broader perception, we will retain empathy and come out of every situation with love for ourselves and others.

People take their existence too seriously. Therefore, we complicate our own lives. In fact, life is quite easy if we learn to let go of the unhealthy side of our ego.

It is understandable that as we grow up, we need to constantly learn. In fact, a person should learn throughout his life because it significantly improves brain function, slows down aging, and can reduce the risk of developing Alzheimer's disease. However, eternal learning has taught us to use only the intellect. Intelligence is a good thing, but it is only necessary for survival. Intelligence is like an object, a weapon, but in order to work with it, you must also have knowledge and feelings. Using only the intelligence created by the "ego," we will constantly build a wall around ourselves, higher and higher, and want to protect ourselves every time we encounter criticism or even a compliment. The "ego" thinks that everything someone says to him is directed against him, and listening to an ordinary opinion can become another reason for defense, outburst of anger, aggression.

The opposite of 'ego' is being. It is being in the moment and looking at what is happening through being in the here and now rather than the past. For example, our being would never look at the world through envy. Imagine - you wake up and run outside to be the first to breathe fresh air because you are afraid that there will not be enough for everyone. No way! You breathe calmly, without even thinking (although you should), because even though you can't see the air (!), you still know that it is there, and, most importantly, there will be enough for everyone. You should feel the same peace when thinking about your goals and achieving your dreams. You don't have to stress about it and worry that not everyone will have enough love or material things or anything else where you feel a lack. The world is as abundant with material things as with things like love, air, and a blue sky. Everything is enough for everyone, and everyone has the opportunity to live in abundance, but only if they really want it and it is based on pure intention and not fear or lack. By directing our energy in the right way, we will get what we want.

Behind any negative, destructive emotions that wake up in you due to someone else's actions, there are some past memories of how someone disappointed you, upset you, and disrupted your usual state. You have to understand the same about the other person. You can arouse some emotions in anyone that are unpleasant for him, even though you are not aware of it. Are you starting to feel the importance of empathy now?

In order for any conversation, any discussion to take place, there must be a kind of emptiness in you - a free place where your being is. Being is disconnecting from the past, gender, status, and any other characteristic that limits you in accepting another person. Ideally, this free space should exist in both interlocutors, but you cannot demand it from the other, but only create this openness in yourself. Even then, you will immediately learn to see when the other person starts to feel offended, threatened and starts to speak and hear through his "ego". The suffering we feel is only of our own making.

Let's imagine that you send an e-mail, a day, two, five have passed, but you still haven't received an answer. How will you act? Will you start thinking through your "ego," grow anger in yourself and build a wall around yourself, thinking - he has not answered me! How dare he! I'm not going to pray! In this way, you begin to cultivate this offended "ego" in yourself and believe that everything is happening against you, although in reality you have not clarified all the circumstances. Maybe this person doesn't answer because he is sick or on a long vacation, or simply the e-mail address was not correct, or the letter went

HOW TO LEARN TO ACCEPT
YOURSELF AND OTHERS

1 | Don't expect anything from others - you yourself know what you need and want the most, so always express your desires loudly and clearly, and don't wait for someone to guess them on their own.

2 | Give only as much as the other person is ready to receive, and don't get upset if it's less than what you really want to give. Everything has its time.

3 | Get for yourself what you want. Taking care of your own well-being is not vanity; you have to prioritize yourself because only then can you take care of others. Both in childhood and in later years, we are taught that if you don't share, you are conceited, greedy, or only thinking of yourself, etc. The difference is that we don't have to share with everyone who asks. We need to assess who genuinely needs it and then share. Remember the people who play the victim card, always making you feel guilty for having more than them. Don't fall into this trap and remember that everyone has exactly what they need in life, and the key is to understand that everyone determines how much they receive. There is enough for everyone, just like air!

4 | Approach every situation from at least two points of view. Imagine that life is a movie - what scenarios are possible for one plot?

LYING

Have you ever lied or caught someone lying? How did you react at that moment? How did your "ego" feel? The point is that we lie when we are not completely satisfied with what we have done in a given situation. It's similar to guilt when we know we should have done something different, but instead of admitting our guilt, the 'ego' chooses to hold on to its version rather than being in the present moment. Can you immediately think of an example from your life? People lie because their 'ego' feels threatened. The second option - because the interlocutor might not be satisfied with the truth. And sometimes it is not related to the conversation partner (or any other person), but to the fact that this person's actions were not in accordance with his being. We may have disappointed someone else by our actions, but most of all ourselves. And what about when someone lies to us? This is where the big turning point begins - because actually... what will change if you know the truth? Maybe accept what the interlocutor tells you as the truth, even if it is a lie? This person is not satisfied with himself, he is already punishing himself! Now he wants you to continue to see the good and true version of him that he wants to be. You don't have to punish the other person for lying; he already does it to himself. Think about who are the people from whom you hide your imperfections? Strangers or your own? Probably yours, because in their eyes you want to be the best. And it's the same with the people close to you - why can someone lie to you? Because they feel threatened and actually want you to continue to see the best version of them that they want you to see.

And what do we care? Only those who are dear to us, important, whom we want to protect and preserve. What can be concluded from this? That if someone lies to you, you can be grateful, because obviously you are so dear to this person that he wants to spoil your image of himself. Instead of getting angry, remember that he is not satisfied with himself. No, I do not support lying, but I have realized that it is easier to accept a lie because the other person already knows that he did something wrong. I know this must be a very unpopular opinion, and I will always stand for telling the truth, whatever that may be. But I hope that it will help someone to understand the other's narrow thinking through the fearful "ego" and the choice to withhold the truth.

Empathy is one of those qualities
that should neither be increased
nor eradicated.
It needs to be balanced.

Too much empathy and being overly sensitive and understanding make a person very susceptible to the moods of other people. This makes it difficult to distance ourselves from the suffering of others, and it's challenging to disconnect from external emotions, work, world events, and other factors beyond our control. The main problem with being particularly sensitive is that it's hard for a person to remain indifferent, and it disrupts the functioning of the nervous system. However, it's worth remembering that it's not your job to justify someone's actions or solve someone else's problem. Understand that when you take responsibility, you take it away from someone else. But there are situations when it is necessary to allow others to answer for their actions and learn from their mistakes. Balancing empathy will be a tool that helps you evaluate how to better react to various situations that come from the external environment. You have to be able to listen to other people's problems and express supportive words, but you have to be able to separate them from yourself and not let foreign emotions into your body that take away your energy. Then you expose yourself to the possibility of attracting various energy drainers.

EMPATHS AND THEIR "FRIENDS"

Have you ever been in such company (even with just one person) that you felt exhausted? Conversely, have you ever attended a lengthy, more tiring event that left you feeling recharged? For any meeting to be productive, there needs to be an exchange of energy. But this can only occur if a person is "pure" — if they give from themselves what is their being and receive from the other what is the purity and sincerity of the other person. Whatever it is, even when meeting a stranger, if they are genuine and you are the same, there will be an exchange of energy, which can sometimes be even greater than with a person you have known for a long time, who does not show their true self, hiding behind their egocentrism, in this way, giving nothing of oneself and not wanting to receive what the other gives.

The electromagnetic field around a person attracts what it emits and what needs what is emitted. An empath's "friends" (read: enemies) are energy drainers who do this relatively consciously, thus "feeding" themselves without giving anything in return. They can also be called energy vampires or energy-informational parasites, although in my opinion, this type of people would not deserve a specific designation because they are not completely on their own; they try to get energy from those from whom it is easy to receive it. Their goal is to put the "victim" in the center, make them feel valued, but then slowly, gradually lead their "ego" to the desired outcome.

The more a person complains about something or someone, the better it makes them feel. The "ego" feels satisfied.

When it is time to turn to oneself again, such a person refuses to listen to their nature, evaluates themselves only by their physical body, appearance, and material things, and is empty again — without energy and ready to look for the next victim. The more fulfilled a person is, the less they need things around them, bought pleasures, and other people. As an empath learns to control their energy and not give it to people who want to "feed" themselves and their "ego" in this way, this energy drainer will feel that their "supplier" is no longer generous and will look for a new one. This is the reason why there are people who often change partners or are constantly looking for new friendships; they are looking for new "givers" to get energy from the new source.

Energo-informational parasites also tend to do "transmitter" programming. Don't worry; it's not related to any spells but only to getting into your mind, your thinking. This programming can happen as an artificial elevation of one's significance, importance, thus making the other person feel smaller and, as it were, subordinate, tied down because they themselves no longer know or know anything. This can take the form of perpetually asking a parent for advice, for example, because that parent has programmed from childhood that only their opinion is the right one. A programmed person behaves like a puppet; they are not in control of their life because they are exposed to the energy-informational parasite.

He is programmed not to think, thus becoming a light energy giver. We must learn to separate our energy from the energy of society; otherwise, we will only continue to obey everyone else. That is why it is important to learn to control this giving of energy because we can give it to the wrong person, and not to the one who would be ready to really give a good charge of energy in return. A programmed person lives according to alien programs and alien minds and acts according to alien will.

The classic trick of energy-informative parasites and energy vampires is to put you as if in the center, in the main place, and then act in such a way as to achieve the desired outcome. "I'm doing it for you!" and "I just want you better!" are the classic programmer's arguments. This co-dependence can also be programmed from the other side—putting not yourself but the "victim" in the main role, as if saying, "You have to help me because only you can do it!" or "I don't have anyone else who can do it..." and so on. This behavior of the energy sucker is clear manipulation, which will continue until the energy source itself does not stop it. However, often the "source" is afraid to break this connection because they are intimidated or feel guilty. If one understood the immediate freedom one would gain by severing this unhealthy bond, half the work would be done.

Think about it - what decisions have you made that someone else took because "it will be better for you"? By breaking the connection with the energy suckers, they will find a new "source" for themselves because they will understand that you have "exposed" their actions and will no longer allow themselves to be manipulated. It is very likely that you will then feel guilty, especially if it was a close person or even a family member. However, it is possible that this kind of action is necessary for this person to understand that it is much more valuable to reveal one's being and create one's energy to share and then receive the other's pure energy in return.

I believe and know that every person is good, but often he has moved so far away from his essence that he has lost his "center" that he no longer knows how to independently create the energy he needs. Break the emotional ties with your energy drainer, and you will very likely clear the way to their being!

In fact, if a person is whole, there is no need for anyone else. Then the individual is solid in its center.

NARCISSISTS

Narcissistic behavior is a mental condition in which people have an exaggerated sense of self-importance, a deep need for constant attention and admiration, anxious relationships, and a lack of empathy for others. Narcissism involves thinking completely through your ego and accepting that everything that happens is about you. When they hear criticism, narcissists defend themselves by blaming someone else, and this blaming never ends in any situation. The crazy thing is that narcissists are often self-aware of this theatrics, but their "ego" is so big that they can't do anything else because they think that if they won't do it to you, you will definitely do it to them! This is why they choose to turn on their "ego" again and again and build a wall, waiting for you to make a mistake so that they can bring you down and feel better about themselves.

If you are an empath and often find yourself in situations where you are criticized for what you do, or when you do things for others but are never good enough, then it is very likely that you have had to deal with narcissists. How to recognize them? Almost nothing. Only after you have expended energy trying to satisfy the narcissist, will you be drained and abandoned, and only then will you feel it and understand it. Unfortunately, in the beginning, when you learn to recognize such narcissistic behavior, this can be your experience. However, there are some ways to recognize a narcissist early on. The word "contact" should be understood as communication, interaction, and social perception in any kind of relationship - family, work, private relationships, friends - anywhere. If these are people we know during our life, for example, as adults, then at first it may seem like the most charismatic, the most beautiful person in the whole room, who catches your attention among the rest of the people with just a glance, and it seems that already at that moment they know how much they will drain you.

The actions of narcissistic people are dictated by their 'ego' and complete lack of empathy. It's your choice to accept or let this person go.

Some signs to recognize a narcissist in any type of relationship:

- Tries to twist your words or claims that you said/did something that you didn't actually say or do.

- Controls the relationship and expects that everything you do will be subordinated to them.

- Reschedules meetings, changes plans sometimes without even informing you.

- Ignores your wishes/requests/needs.

- The difference between self-disclosure and narcissism is they build relationships around their problems.

- Never tells about their plans.

- Says one thing, does another.

- Feels uncomfortable for others on important days (for example, a birthday) because it is not "their day," they are not the center of attention, so they may not even attend the celebration, or they may assign an important role to themselves in the celebration, for example, by actively initiating games or undertaking the preparation of decorations, etc.

- Always smiles to others, but in your presence, this mask falls, for incomprehensible reasons the person suddenly changes and maybe even starts to blame you for something that happened when you were among people, where you supposedly "humiliated" them.

- Places too much emphasis on external appearance (both for themselves and for their partner - values are based on "ego," not being).

To better understand a narcissist, learn not to get hung up on their words, whether future-oriented or past-oriented. Live in the present and hear them each time as if for the first time, but sometimes choose not to hear them at all because, in reality, the narcissist did not genuinely mean those words. In their thoughts, they might have intended to say something different than what actually came out in physical form. They didn't say those words to communicate with you, but rather to satisfy their ego. It may sound absurd, but when faced with such a situation, you will understand. If your love language is words and speech, like mine, then this can be very challenging, but turning on empathy not only in such situations but also in general is mandatory. People with narcissistic traits did not choose to be narcissists; it is not a free choice. They have become prisoners of the fortification of their "ego," from which they can no longer break free on their own, sinking into an ever deeper "mess." Narcissism is often a result of parenting, and at least one parent has had this "altered" mindset. Therefore, the child inherits it because the past has taught them that constant self-protection is necessary, or they will have to suffer.

Narcissists don't live in the present; they live in the past. They believe that if they do not defend themselves or hurt others first, they will be hurt themselves—their present and future "ego."

Most often, individuals with narcissistic tendencies grow up with parents who excessively attend to their needs while neglecting the child. Consequently, as adults, these individuals may "punish" their friends, loved ones, and partners in the same way they were punished as children. Alternatively, narcissistic traits may arise from the opposite parenting style, where a child is granted everything they desire, leading them to believe that everything is meant only for them. If they don't receive what they think they deserve, someone is to blame, and it is done "intentionally." Narcissism can also result from past relationships where the partner was narcissistic, and the person did not realize it, giving too much of themselves. After a breakup, they may adopt a narcissistic attitude as a defense mechanism, preventing them from opening up and giving in future relationships out of fear of being used again.

Regardless of the reasons, narcissists cannot be changed, but they can be shown the love that every human being deserves. Love is a broad concept and should not be limited to understanding only as closeness in a partnership. It involves accepting the other being. Therefore, it's crucial to recognize that this discussion is not limited to romantic relationships but applies to friendships, colleagues, neighbors, etc. It's very likely that narcissists will themselves realize over time that they are living in captivity. At that point, they may desire to change because they will grow tired of their limited thinking and restricted life through the "ego." Until that happens, learn to expand your perception and activate empathy.

And no, not every person has some part of a narcissist. Only a narcissist can think like that while trying to justify himself. It's worth thinking about.

EMOTIONAL INTELLIGENCE

Emotional intelligence is the ability to understand, use, and control one's emotions, leading them to a positive outcome, stress relief, effective communication, empathy, and conflict avoidance. Several parts of the brain are responsible for emotional intelligence, cooperating with each other - the ventromedial prefrontal cortex and frontal cortex, and the amygdala and the nucleus accumbens. It's like a very fast teamwork - creating tactics in a stressful situation when you have to react to everything simultaneously - emotions, logic, sensitivity - and express it verbally while keeping your body calm.

It is no surprise that emotional intelligence is at a relatively low level today, and empathy is not developed as a result. Emotional intelligence focuses on the conversation, building a dialogue with the interlocutor in the best way for both. It is not a monologue or manipulation with the desire to achieve a solution that suits you. Emotional intelligence is unequivocally about letting go of your superego, but it also requires being in complete control of your mind in the present moment and acting in accordance with your individuality.

There are many recommendations on how to develop emotional intelligence, where it is recommended to start by being aware of how you react to people, how you react in stressful situations, and evaluate how your actions will affect others, etc. It's all doable, but it would be best if you start thinking before you get into these situations. Create your own communication style and follow it! Define the values of your speech.

For example: positive, open, kind. Assess how you want to react and practice the first words you will say, for example, when someone gives you criticism or advice that you really don't want to receive. For example, "Thanks, I hadn't thought of that, I'll look into it!" or "Thanks for the suggestion, but I get them so often that I still have to figure out what the best solution would be!". Change your thinking by preparing for different situations. Then, if you make a habit of preparing the first answers to unpleasant questions, you will reduce your stress and the desire to react impulsively. Respectively, you will train your body to keep calm because this situation will not surprise you if you have prepared for it in time. Conflicts arise because we speak impulsively, without thinking in the present.

Emotional intelligence is not about responding nicely. There is no point in lying to the interlocutor and saying what you don't mean at all just to look good, correct, or pretty, but to "fry" and "boil" inside, and then display it all at home to your loved ones because it has to be displayed somewhere. Emotional intelligence is formed when you really say what you think, and you don't need to discuss it with someone behind your back, vent your anger, or talk down to the specific person. It will only be pretend! It takes real work with yourself and the ability to accept that someone else may be right, or you can try to understand the other person and support your opinion with arguments that would dispel his doubts even if they are not said out loud. People themselves don't even realize what the real reason for their doubts is, so you can help them find it by asking simple questions to better understand their point of view, instead of immediately countering yours just to prove yourself right. It is rare that there is really only one correct opinion. By looking deeper into each situation, you can not only expand your vision but also, perhaps, find an even better solution that you had not thought of until now. But you really have to think about it - not to give in for the sake of dear peace and then go to the gym angry, to put your pent-up energy somewhere. This is, of course, a better solution than shouting everything at your partner, but by training emotional intelligence, you will make your life significantly easier by understanding the current situation, putting yourself in the other person's shoes, and using empathy to steer the conversation in the most beneficial direction for both.

Emotional intelligence is the ability to recognize one's own and the interlocutor's emotions. First, deal with your own emotions, and then quickly find a way, based on the conversation partner's emotions, to convey your message in the best way for both.

It's not about indulging the interlocutor; it's about showing courtesy and understanding to have a meaningful conversation. You might ask, why do you have to do this? Why should you be that welcoming, understanding, empathetic interlocutor? The answer is quite simple. Someone has to start! Society is already sick with misunderstanding, resentment, and fear-filled thinking. It is almost impossible to have productive conversations and express your opinion without balanced empathy. And conversation, communication, is one of the most important basic things that we have on a daily basis. Only by being open about our intentions and learning to adapt to the interlocutor, without offending him, can we have a full conversation. And what if this is also the key to reducing technology use in society?

NAIVETY

What do you think about naive people? Is this a sign of weakness or a positive trait? Do you have a person in mind, or maybe you think you are naive?

Naivety can manifest itself as believing everything you are told and the ability to see only the good in a person. Isn't that a good feature? Then how did the idea arise that "he is naive after all..." or "she naively believes that..."? In fact, naivety as a term by which to judge another person exists only for those who seek their own superiority. I will explain. If I believe everything I'm told, am I naive or trusting? If I believe that there is something good in every person, am I naive or hopeful? If I know I can achieve anything I want, am I naive or determined? Everyone chooses how to think, but it must be said that naivety as a concept is only for those who hide behind the ego and do not live according to their "I". For those who are completely themselves, such a concept does not exist; instead, they are truly loving, loyal, purposeful, reliable, etc. He who is angry and dissatisfied with himself will find something to be angry and dissatisfied with in another. He who loves and accepts himself will always accept and find something to love in the other. But this is not naivety. And yes, I truly believe that there is something good in every person. But it hides somewhere behind the big "ego" and just needs to be shaken and "thrown" into unprecedented conditions and made to enjoy unusual experiences that will expand his perception.

Perception cannot be expanded by speaking or listening. It can only be extended by doing.

The body's emotional experience is what determines how much we will easily be able to put ourselves in the other person's skin in our thoughts and look at the situation from different perspectives and points of view to understand as closely as possible the actions and motives of the other.

PRACTICES FOR EXPANDING PERCEPTION AND BALANCING EMPATHY

Travel - Although travel may sound like a leisurely or budget-busting trip, it can actually offer much more than just flashy impressions of tourist spots. In my opinion, there are two types of travel – firstly, getting to know a new culture, and secondly, getting to know yourself. Whichever way you choose, both will broaden your perception. Every city, every country, no matter how close it is to your home, is a little different. Its inhabitants are shaped by a nation's history, weather, economic status, and as these are only some of the criteria, no two places are identical. Therefore, it is especially interesting to get to know other cultures, which will significantly expand your thinking. But the second way - traveling to get to know yourself - involves being in unusual positions for your body, such as traveling with a backpack, sleeping in the open air, or, on the contrary, going on trips with a tour group - anything that does not correspond to your classic trip. Any type of travel is good if done with a purpose. It is interesting that people choose to "relax" abroad during their vacations because we can "relax" at home or by the lake at any time! That's why, in my opinion, foreign countries are often underestimated, and we take too much of ourselves with us when we travel, leaving no free space for getting to know a new culture, society, or ourselves.

Community service - Donating money or things to those who need them more is good, of course, but frankly, I think we comfort ourselves instead of getting to the root of the problem. It's good work and inner peace of mind, but people don't always need new things. You can also donate your time, share your energy. When I was young, playing drums in a girl band, we thought of doing an acoustic concert at Christmas and going to orphanages to give the kids a little Christmas concert. It was so exciting! Often, the children recognized that this was what they needed, not big boxes and piles of clothes. In some places, one of the rooms of the orphanage, full of unsorted piles of clothes on the tables, looked a bit like long-forgotten humpals. By giving the children a concert at Christmas and then staying for a little party and making friends, we evoked unprecedented feelings in them and in ourselves. Conversations with children who have grown up in different circumstances definitely gave a different perspective. No matter how sad life is without parents, they were there for each other! And this most often continues even after the orphanage - these children stick together and support each other, and the fact that the beginning of their life was spent in an orphanage does not necessarily mean that the rest of their lives will be difficult. Of course, often these children become involved in criminal activities because they want to belong to a group and do not realize the consequences, but there are also many successful examples.

But you can learn about them only by being nearby and getting to know this environment, in order to understand that in reality, children in orphanages do not always feel bad. Yes, they don't have the easiest start in life, but that doesn't mean they can't make the sequel the way they want it to be. Coming back to the donation and community work - what I want to encourage - instead of just sympathizing, get to know and learn about the "problem" closer! Whether it is a nursing home for the elderly, or an orphanage, or Africa - form your own opinion when you enter this environment, and you will also see something beautiful there, which is perhaps not in your everyday life. Remember that each of us is given as much as we can bear in this life. If you have the opportunity to help someone - great! Just do it by asking directly what the person would most like today. Maybe it's just talk and not something tangible.

3 | New content - Expand your perception with literature that is completely unusual for you, for example, a biographical book, or a documentary film about a significant person in history, or anything else that is outside the content you consume on a daily basis. Try to imagine the relevant events and think, what can you learn from the relevant people and events? What qualities do you see in how you would act in relevant situations? The world is filled with valuable people and events; get to know them!

AFFIRMATIONS FOR EMPATHY AND PERCEPTION

I am delighted to assist those who seek my help and genuinely need it.

I attentively listen to other people's stories.

I enjoy learning about history, exploring various cultures, and understanding different religions to enhance my comprehension of the world.

I value honesty and express my thoughts while remaining considerate of my conversation partner.

I extend empathy even towards those with whom I disagree.

Feeling others' emotions doesn't make me responsible for them.

Kindness is a gift that costs nothing but can achieve a lot.

I choose to explore the world to broaden my perspective and make my daily life more interesting.

I effortlessly and joyfully expand my perception.

Although I comprehend and feel the pain of others, I can distance myself from it.

I am grounded in my center.

I relish traveling and seeing the world from new perspectives.

I aim to understand people without passing judgment.

My perception effortlessly broadens. I enjoy asking questions to learn about people and the world.

I know how to separate my energy from other people's problems.

***

MATURE!

What is respect? What do you respect, and what do you not? How do you know when you respect someone, and how do you recognize when they respect you? If we exclude the usual expressions of kindness and formalities, what does respect truly mean? Is it the acceptance of another person's words, actions, decisions, opinions, even when you don't agree with them? Yes, probably. However, one cannot help but feel that this is too superficial to sufficiently define the word "respect." Talking and expressing an opinion is so easy! There are people who are natural storytellers, speaking non-stop and very persuasively. You have to listen and nod along in agreement because what is said sounds so convincing that it seems like they definitely know what they are talking about. Then, your opinion becomes less important, as out of respect for the other's convincing position, there is seemingly no room for further discussion. At least, that's what I used to think. Anyone delivering a compelling monologue? Okay, good! Then I will comply. Until something changed.

I guess I'm starting to grow up, and with my 30 years of life experience, I'm beginning to see the flaws in these convincing monologues. I've started to see people from their true side and understand that often these reassuring words have no meaning; they are empty, just beautiful thanks. This realization came when a specific topic was so close to me that I had gained more experience to share and defend my point of view, as it was more complete, and I was 100% and even more convinced of my correctness. Of course, there is no single truth. Everyone has their own vision, but you can only have such a vision if you have gone through something and felt everything on your skin, down to the finest details. Otherwise, it is not an experience. Can an opinion be objective if you don't know what you're talking about? Can you share your opinion based only on your thoughts? An opinion should always be based on some experience from which a personal lesson has been learned. A reasoned opinion on how to act next time, what to change, to do better is built on it. An opinion obtained only through personal experience is valuable because there is no other such opinion, and it is not comparable to an opinion expressed on the basis of generally known facts. The only question is who will present his truth more convincingly.

I started thinking about who the people I truly respect are and why. First, of course, parents come to mind. Without hypocrisy, it's hard to imagine anything better that I could have chosen when I was born. It is said that children choose their parents. Well then, I can be very satisfied with my first life choice. My parents have set an excellent example both with their long life together and by creating a beautiful environment. They've demonstrated virtue through their work and, of course, by raising us - two great daughters. Support has always been received, even though sometimes it took the form of stricter parenting. Either way, our big wishes and choices have always been respected and supported. I admire their calm acceptance of my ideas and decisions. The next step is in my hands - how much responsibility do I take to continue the chosen path? This is the example of my parents and the biggest reason for respect - respect for your child and their wishes, even though it may seem that "the little one doesn't understand anything." The best thing that parents can give, in addition to love, is trust and support without reproaches if things do not go as they would like.

In my circle of friends and acquaintances, there are also people who, with their great ambitions, strong faith, and deter-mination, have created and successfully manage companies worth millions. Is it the money that made me think of them? Let's call them successes, and yes, they can be measured in different ways. But they are also united by hard, persistent work and a strong belief in what they do. But that's not all. These are only the visible parts. Only by being close to people can you get to know their values and intentions. And all these people also possess loyalty, humanity, familiality, and naturalness. Aren't these wonderful qualities? Do you have them? How they treat any person and their family is a great value in my eyes. You can make a lot of money, but what good does it do if you treat fellow uman beings who have not yet reached the same financial level as you with disrespect? Probably, then your interaction with those around you will change - it is not for nothing that they say that money changes a person. Especially if you have been there once and know how difficult it is to break out of the usual rhythm of work-salary-bills-work. Not everyone can do that! And maybe it's even good that it is, because the world is really full of self-interest seekers who, as soon as they receive the first big addition to their bank account, immediately forget the first moral principle - every person is valuable as they are. There are people who would use this money for selfish or even evil purposes, rather than to create something great, something that would change the world and have a significant impact on our future.

We could not and probably would not even want to be on this planet alone. That's why you respect everyone and especially those closest to you.

There is another person whom I have great respect for. Someone who has been an incredible support to me through some really tough times in my life, for which I will be forever grateful. And although I could list many good qualities, I value his patience the most. Peace and knowing that everything is happening as it should. Whatever happens in the future and whatever has happened in the past, every day I understand more and more how important it is to appreciate the other person today. Getting angry about the past is pointless, worrying about the future is unnecessary. Therefore, learning patience and being in the present allows you to better appreciate what you have now instead of lamenting what could have been.

Learn to love another persons uniqueness. It creates a harmony that you would not achieve alone, and that is why in any relationship the other person has something that you yourself lack. When you learn to notice and accept it, then you are truly able to appreciate, respect, and love the other's unique nature.

Putting people next to each other, I started looking for connections, which is what creates respect for people. I realize I walk a very fine line when it comes to respect. However, I would like to emphasize that, in my opinion, this word "respect" does not have an opposite. We cannot judge, condemn, or even teach anyone. That's why I don't say respect and disrespect. Don't think of this as 'black or white'. Even if the opposite is called "disrespect," it does not mean to be unkind, to ignore, to insult. No one has the right to judge another. It's just that there are people who show themselves as human beings through words and actions, which creates reverence for them and greater respect. It forces acceptance of these individuals, despite the incompatibility of opinions, strange character traits, and other characteristics that may be different from the average society. We should respect every person, and I believe that as soon as we work more on ourselves and return to our essence, it will happen. As soon as we are not ourselves and hide behind "masks" or are afraid to be authentic, it already shows that you yourself are afraid of your true nature and do not allow others to see (therefore also respect) your true "me"!

We all have our own path to follow in life. No two experiences or destinies are the same, just as no two people are identical. Everyone has their own values. Life has been more generous to some, less to others, but everyone has the opportunity to shape it the way they want. When a person starts moving towards their goals and takes responsibility, they have to start doing. It's not enough to just study well, read books, or watch TV and express opinions. You really have to learn to do! Doing means thinking, taking risks, getting your hands dirty, putting yourself out there, being persistent, and maybe at times being fearless or at least full of determination. To do, one must learn something or at least have the desire to learn and understand it. If you have a goal you want to achieve, you must also want to understand all the details related to it to know how to achieve this goal better.

This realization made me understand that it is easiest to respect those who have gone through it themselves or at least delved into the details. It is easiest to respect people who have authentic experiences that they live their lives by without forcing others to live the same. They have found their way to a great life, but they don't call it the "only," "right," or "best" way. They do not try to compare themselves with others or judge others by themselves because they know that just as they have created their own lives, so has the other person created theirs. And they respect it!

Respectable people do not judge another person by themselves; they simply respect them. Hearing a true life story about how a person has reached their goal makes you think of the hardships they have gone through, and you want to gasp in admiration that after all that, they are sitting across from me and have achieved so much. Those who are not afraid of work, criticism, and failure. Those for whom the goal is more important than other people's thoughts and empty talk.

Sometimes a person may even do this unconsciously, but this only shows how sincere he is in his intentions and genuine in his actions. People who have gained experience from their actions, carried out based on their feelings, knowledge, and intuition, are, in my opinion, very respectable. You don't have to be a winner or a millionaire to be a leader. The leader comes with his example, experience, and sees it as a value. His recommendations will never be based on the "ego" but on the specific goal. He knows that everyone has his own path to follow, so he is not afraid to share it, just as he is not afraid to breathe, because there will be enough air for all of us.

If a person is not afraid to share his mistakes and is able to look at them from the outside, this is already a sign that he does not put himself first, but his goal. He knows that he has something to achieve, and that it is something bigger and more important than his 'ego'. He is ready to serve his purpose, even if he leaves himself in the background. Who can be more honorable than such a person? A person who fulfills his highest goal and goes for it selflessly. That's how my version of a respectable person came about. This is a person who lives his life to achieve his goal and does not prevent others from doing the same.

Now, about those others - talkers, not doers. About the eternal critics, gossipers, skeptics. Whoever falls into this group, the most important thing is to understand that a person talks badly about another person only to make himself feel better about himself. But these are neither positive, nor productive, nor true thoughts, so it is better not to think at all than to waste your energy on empty talk. That's why gossipers are so boring. Point! I want to devote just such a small paragraph to this ancient topic. And this topic is closed!

to spam. If you constantly think that "he's not answering already" or "I'm not going to call first," or other statements that grow your limited "ego," then you know that you are building a wall around yourself and will constantly want to defend yourself when in reality you could find out the circumstances first and then accept the other's decision, whatever it may be. That's why, expand your perception, balance your empathy, and live in the present.

PRESENT

The "Ego" arises from non-awareness. As soon as you are "triggered" by something and you are aware of it, then you have already started working with your "ego" because, even if you get angry, you notice these emotions of yours. Not being conscious, you will feel not your anger but that the other person is to blame because they try to lower you, offend you, etc. Therefore, to hear your "ego," always be in the present. When you want to react sharply, just stop yourself! Yes, it won't be easy because the anger has escalated, but recognize these moments and wait before hitting back at someone because that's what your 'ego' wants, not your being! Be present and listen to your "ego" so you can manage it.

Why are there questions that you can answer calmly, but when you hear others, you immediately want to react too sharply and explode in anger? Everyone has their own "sensitive" topic. However, if you are aware of this topic, you are already one step ahead and will be able to choose how to react next time. The key is to recognize that you are starting to get angry, and even if you do get angry again, you will know that there is something in you that is speaking through the "ego," and you will be ready to start looking for the cause. It works both ways - even if your interlocutor gets angry, understand that it is his "ego" and do not fight against his anger, but give him time or find the right question that will help you calm down and return to the present moment.

Be aware that by addressing your triggers, you can
significantly improve not only your well-being but
also the quality of communication and relationships
with others.

In life, you have to deal with different people, and communication is inevitable, so you should try to find some positive qualities in each person, not what you would like them to have but, as it turns out, they don't. Learn to get to know each person slowly, rather than judging by the obvious. Learn to want to get to know each person positively! It may take time, yes... But you will gain much more than if you make a judgment ahead of time. What you really need to learn if you want to develop respect is patience. You are so strong with patience! But what exactly is it?

Patience is trusting in
one's inner strength,
knowing that after
hardship will always come ease;
to endure hard
times but still be
grateful.

Patience is the willingness and ability to accept or tolerate events that do not match your vision. Starting with resentment, if you have to wait for others' delays or slow actions (including sitting in traffic jams), with sharing your opinion or knowledge with someone who thinks differently (including communicating with your partner in such a way as not to be offended by the actions or opinions of one or the other, but simply explaining it in a way that the other person can understand) or any other unforeseen problems without becoming annoyed or anxious. Patience is both an emotion and a skill. It can be learned and trained, and the result is when you prioritize thinking over emotion. Patience can significantly improve relationships by preventing hasty, selfish decisions, and harsh words. Patience is also an integral part of empathy, but unlike the ability to empathize with another, respect means accepting the other's point of view based on their experience and sharing that point of view based on your own experience. It definitely has to start with patience.

Maybe they suppressed your desires, didn't allow you to make decisions, or on the contrary - gave you too many options and in the end didn't listen to your choice, and that's why now you feel confused, indecisive, insecure because you still think through your inner child! That's why you lose patience because you want everything now! What would be a healthy contrast? Your inner adult. He knows what he wants, gathers information about the possible choices, makes a decision, and ACTS! An adult always acts. Contrasted with the inner child who waits. It's good to dream, but everyone needs a vision of where they want to go. Patience means going for that vision and not stopping even if any obstacles appear. Patience is respect for yourself and the people who created these unplanned circumstances and being able to accept them because apparently, it was meant to be! Most importantly, keep your vision of where you are going. But stop controlling the circumstances that you cannot influence - a slow queue at the supermarket, a slow co-worker? Why should you waste your energy and get angry at such things?! It's time to mature. Time to let go of the inner child and grow the inner adult. If we don't have a vision of where we want to go, we can very easily "float" downstream. But when you see your destination, even though it is not easy, you will slowly go against the current because you will know that it is the right direction. At that moment, you just have to accept the unexpected and be grateful for what happens to you.

WHY DO WE LOSE PATIENCE?

Standing in a long line with slow service, not getting work done on time from colleagues, nagging your partner, a delayed flight... What are the moments when you get impatient? And have you encountered any of the above things but do not fully associate with yourself? We become impatient when we have set ourselves some tasks or goals. For example, "I have to pick up my child from school in a hurry, why isn't this line moving forward?" or "I want to finish the presentation by Wednesday, but my colleague hasn't given me the information yet." Whenever we have set some inner goal, big or small, but there is an obstacle in the way, we become impatient. In this way, we show disrespect to the other side - the seller who does not serve, in your opinion, fast enough or the people in line who may not be able to count the money or find the payment card. Or a colleague who is late with the transfer of data only because his boss and clients have also created urgent tasks for him. As soon as we go toward the goal and some small obstacle appears in front of us, we become impatient, if we think through our inner child. The inner child wants everything NOW! And fast! I want to! Where is it? Faster! That's what the inner child says. This is another childhood program that we should all review - when we get impatient and what the real reason might be. Then, if we don't have our goals, we flow. We flow gently, we let everything take its course, we swim here and there... At that moment, we are not the determinants of our lives. We are still in our inner child who hopes to receive a miracle without doing anything because "I have to", "I want to"! Maybe you can observe it in yourself when starting a new project or job and hoping for quick success. As soon as you move your little finger, but nothing happens, it throws everything away because "it won't be the same", "I have my principles", "I'm not going to pray". It is the inner child who wants to ignore goal setting, planning, and patience. He thinks that he is always right and that he deserves everything the same way. He is confused, insecure, indecisive. He fluctuates in his desires, because as soon as he does not get one immediately, he turns to the other, thinking that he will get it sooner. Until the end, in the end, it remains in the besh.

Perhaps in childhood, your desires were suppressed, you were not allowed to make decisions, or on the contrary - you were given too many options and in the end did not listen to your choice, and that is why now you feel confused, indecisive, insecure. That's why you lose patience because you want everything now! What would be a healthy contrast? Your inner adult. He knows what he wants, he gathers information about the possible choices, he makes a decision and ACTS! An adult always acts. Contrasted with the inner child who waits. It's good to dream, but everyone needs a vision of where they want to go. Patience means going for that vision and not stopping even if any obstacles appear. Patience is respect for yourself and the people who created these unplanned circumstances and being able to accept them because apparently, it was meant to be! Most importantly, keep your vision of where you are going. But stop controlling the circumstances that you cannot influence - a slow queue at the supermarket, a slow co-worker? Why should you waste your energy and get angry about such things?! It's time to mature. Time to let go of the inner child and grow the inner adult. If we don't have a vision of where we want to go, we can very easily "float" downstream. But when you see your destination, even though it is not easy, you will slowly go against the current because you will know that it is the right direction. At that moment, you just have to accept the unexpected and be grateful for what happens to you.

Imagine that you are wading down a river. It's not fast; it's just inconvenient. The counter-current is not fast, but walking past the big rocks makes it difficult. It happens one by one, and you just want to blame the stones for everything. But... there are rocks in this river! Where else will you sit down and relax when you want to catch your breath? Would a river without any stones really be better? You keep walking, and you see a waterfall ahead. Stand under it for a moment, take in the energetic cold water, and start climbing up the steep bank. Not easy, not fast, but you are patient. Because only a patient person knows that if you keep your inner strength, after any difficulties, something easier will come. Even though your fingers hurt and your feet slip, you keep in mind your destination, which you will reach only by going against the current. You are aware that with every moment, with every small step, you are getting closer to it. You climb to the top of the waterfall, and finally, an amazing view opens up! The river here is very wide and very shallow with soft sand and no stones; you can literally run along it! You wonder how good it is that you kept climbing instead of going downstream with the many uncomfortable rocks. As you smoothly walk down the river, it becomes a little deeper, but still calm. And who would have thought it - you meet a boatman! He's heading in the same direction as you and kindly offers to take you a bit. You are sitting in the same boat, and in gratitude for the transport, you offer to row in his place. The boatman, surprised to have met such a pleasant travel companion, gives you his compass so that you will continue to know the right direction. You say goodbye when the river almost disappears into the gorgeous greenery. The birds are chirping, the air is fresh, and after a few more steps along the river, you are overwhelmed with excitement. You know that you have reached your destination - even though there are a few as happy goal achievers as you, all of them have passed through the same river and welcome you with warmth and understanding. You look back at the river and imagine what it would have been like to flow along the stream, where many people are going, hitting rocks past each other and ending up in a common big bath where you disappear... You are grateful for this journey you have experienced. Be glad you were so patient and respect everyone you meet because you know they went through the same thing.

You never know what you will meet on your way, but learn not to see the unexpected as a hindrance. Do not attach importance to obstacles and do not focus your energy on them unnecessarily. Learn to think differently.

You have to choose a destination, but you have to stop thinking about who there will be a way. Learn to accept the decision but do not try to control circumstances. Change your thinking and realize that with each step you are closer to your destination. Just be patient and respect yourself and others.

DIFFERENT THINKING

As soon as you encounter something unexpected that causes you resentment, irritation, anger, or any other emotion that makes you impatient and disrespectful, learn to choose one of these three different ways of thinking:

11 ACCEPTANCE. When we plan things, we think we know what the best outcome is, right? And then when something goes wrong or just doesn't go as planned, we feel depressed and sad. What if it really wasn't meant for you? What if failure really is the best outcome? Before evaluating the situation as "good" or "bad," ask yourself - is it worth thinking about it at all? Maybe you can accept it and move forward, focusing on something new and positive? If we constantly think about a problem, we direct our energy there. This is how the problem grows, not the solution. Instead, we can focus on something positive and new, and that's why this decision will create the kind of energy that will actually attract something positive and new! If you also call an event a "problem," try to forget about it at least for a day or a week and check if it is still a problem after that. Maybe it will have already been resolved? Accepting a problem does not mean giving up; it means you refuse to fight because fighting drains your energy. Where your focus goes, there your energy flows.

NEUTRALITY. If, however, you cannot accept the "problem" and still know that the outcome must be different, then decide to start acting again - at the point where you are now. Remain neutral and simply choose to make this moment your new 'beginning.' The goal remains the same, the past is forgotten and this is now the new starting point. This means that you do not judge what happened as good or bad; you simply choose to become neutral and start "from scratch" in the current circumstances. You accept the current conditions and choose to continue directing your energy towards your desired goal.

ACTION. You are the owner of your body and you choose where to direct your energy, so whenever you feel that the result is not what you imagined and you feel that you can do it better/differently/correctly, then start from the beginning and try to avoid your previous mistakes! You choose where to focus your energy, so if you feel you could have done something better, go back to the beginning and start doing it! Evaluate - what is it that you want to change? Remember that you can fix and change anything you want if you make that decision and keep the faith and 100% determination to do it. Sometimes we don't hit the "goal" the first time, not because it's not for us, but because we're not ready for it yet. So learn from your mistakes and make the decision to start over again if you feel that you still have to get to the destination you wanted in the beginning.

The key word in applying divergent thinking is decision! Decide and act! By procrastinating in making a decision, you are not training patience, but you are depriving yourself of energy! There is no right or wrong decision. Even if you make what you think is the wrong decision, there is a chance that sooner or later you will reach the same destination as the other option, just by gaining some kind of lesson that will be useful to you later in life.

Remember - ask yourself the necessary questions, evaluate the information received, and make a quick decision so that you can act quickly! The inner child is unproductive because it doesn't act, so your patience is running out! But the inner adult is productive because he applies different thinking and action. Your task is to move away from thinking about the problem as quickly as possible because, in this way, you will waste an unnecessary amount of energy. Especially if it's something where you feel guilty or angry - these are low vibrational qualities that greatly reduce your energy. Take small steps in the direction of the decision you made, and you will see that once your focus changes, everything will fall into place quickly.

If we once patiently wait for flowers, trees, berries that grow slowly, then why can't we wait for people? We respect nature, but why don't we look at people with the same respect and with patience?

GRATITUDE

What if everything we encountered in our lives was worthy of joy? For example, a conversation with an elderly person— not everyone has the opportunity to learn about what happened 70 years ago! Or sitting in rush hour—what better excuse to listen to a podcast a little longer before heading home? Or a flat car tire—so you had to stop. What if we respected every person and event we encountered along the way, knowing that it would somehow bring us some positive outcome? The usual pile of dirty clothes is received with joy—we are active in our family, we do everything, we play sports, we live; that's why there are so many dirty clothes! Sound funny? But it really works! Every thing can be looked at through a positive prism. And you will ask—why would it be necessary?

Man, like everything else in nature, consists of energy. Qualities such as gratitude and joy raise high vibrations in us—this means that the heart center opens, which works coherently with the mind. In this state, we become magnets for all that is good! We radiate joy, which means that we automatically attract the same to ourselves! Then, if we feel shame, guilt, or fear in our heart, we are the opposite of giving—on the contrary, we seem to absorb everything into ourselves, thus attracting the same "sucking" events to us, but the positive ones don't even come close to us! That's why it's so important to raise your vibration right now in gratitude for all that you have. Already at the beginning of the book, we talked about the fact that the vibrations of the universe are currently changing. So understand your role here. Be aware that the Sun is electric, the Earth is magnetic, and you are in the middle of both; therefore, you are electromagnetic! Expand your electromagnetic field with coordinated heart and mind action to share joy and attract it to you in the future! We would make life easier for ourselves if we started to think differently and learn to be thankful for every person we meet, every "lesson" we receive, and simply for everything good that happens to us today.

Make up your mind, act, and
be patient because
behind every difficulty
comes ease.

The measure of my patience during a long-term depressive state was fulfilled when I couldn't tie my shoes. They were very simple shoelaces intended to tie a straightforward knot, but the eruption of emotions within me at that time made me realize that this is not normal. The shoes are not to blame! I'm not guilty! What is happening in my mind and body to evoke these emotions in me? While there have been crazier incidents than this, the emotional tipping point when I lost control of my anger was triggered by such a simple everyday task. Not all the most psychologically challenging events are worth mentioning, as the most difficult thing will vary for everyone. Nevertheless, those shoelaces became a valuable reference point for me, teaching me not only to be patient in everyday things but to control my emotions, my mind, my speech, and my actions in general. It's all achievable! And not just to control or suppress but to truly understand the best course of action in each moment. I have never liked to complain or "bicker" about anything; it is not my natural state. Yes, I can become passionate and enthusiastic about what I'm doing, but it's a form of passion. Learn to control your mind and your emotions, and you will find much more love for yourself.

PRACTICES FOR DEVELOPING PATIENCE

BREATHING - Monks are taught from a young age (starting at the age of five) that the first thing to learn in monk school is breathing. We are born with breath, and we will leave with breath. All major emotions in our lives are experienced through breath – joy, excitement, anger, anxiety, and others. Therefore, conscious and correct breathing is essential for mastering control over our physical and mental bodies. The primary condition for proper breathing is to breathe exclusively through the nose. The human mouth is designed for eating, while the nose acts as a filter. It serves as the body's initial "defense mechanism" against pollution and germs, warms the air we breathe, and helps us receive about 20% more oxygen compared to breathing through the mouth. Breathing impacts the entire human body, affecting heartbeat, blood circulation, digestion, and brain activity. Incorrect breathing puts the body in a state of stress. Efficient breathing involves taking fewer breaths for more oxygen, achievable through nose breathing. Slow, deep, rhythmic breaths increase lung capacity, a crucial factor for longevity, and help keep the body in a restful state. Proper breathing is easy to practice consciously. Learn to slow down your breathing consciously to make quick progress in calming your anxious mind. Unconscious breath-holding is common among office workers and can stress the body, but conscious breath-holding can be beneficial, increasing carbon dioxide levels and teaching the body

2 | POSTURE - Daily hunching leads to forward-pulled shoulders, contracted lungs, and accelerated breathing, signaling a stressful situation to the body. Correct posture, like proper breathing, is essential for feeling secure and maintaining slow, steady breathing throughout the day.

3 | PHYSICAL ACTIVITY - Running, yoga, and exercise significantly reduce anxiety symptoms, promoting a calm mind and increased patience. Even a single run can alter brain chemistry in the prefrontal cortex responsible for cognitive function. Outdoor activities provide fresh air and sunlight, known depression-relievers. This brain "organization" enhances mental clarity, decision-making, reduces impulsivity, and increases focus. Introducing regular physical activity into daily life improves sleep quality, addressing long-term stress caused by insufficient sleep. Taking responsibility for yourself and incorporating physical activity, even three times a week, can positively impact sleep patterns. Embrace this rewarding practice for a more pleasant experience.

4 | BODY DETOX: It's not just about nutrition! There are different types of detox, and their primary function is to eliminate dangerous, harmful substances from the body. Running is a form of detox, just like going to the sauna. Other types include nasal irrigation or Jala Neti, foot detox, oxygen detox, and more. However, in this discussion, the focus will be on the food we consume.

With numerous opinions and discoveries about nutrition, it's challenging to discern what to believe and choose. In my view, if a person has put their body in order, released old, accumulated energy, and consciously strives to care for their body for long-term health, they will instinctively know what their body needs. Nevertheless, there are some important aspects to consider about this "feeling." Often, our cravings are influenced by the bacteria residing in our bodies, demanding the familiar foods we've grown accustomed to since childhood. Ideally, the human body is designed to absorb fruits, seeds, and nuts. When the body is deprived of its accustomed foods, the bacteria signal cravings for meat, warm potatoes, etc. This perspective on proper nutrition raises the question of whether human hands, designed for taking, plucking, and opening things, were intended for digging or hunting. Understanding the fundamental function of refreshment, which is based on nourishing the body, was a revelation. Initiating self-cleansing and self-renewal, refreshing mirrors nature's processes. Therefore, specialists recommend consuming fruits, berries, and melons for nerve problems, as they contain everything the body needs for quicker restoration and stabilization. Sickness often signals the need for a cleansing process. Regular detoxification prevents toxin accumulation, promoting longer cell life and maintaining youthfulness. Toxins accumulated in the body contribute to wrinkle formation and initiate various diseases, emphasizing the importance of reviewing one's menu for a cleaner, healthier body.

5| Initially considering these changes as absurd, I've come to appreciate the ease and energy derived from a menu of fruits, berries, and nuts. Gradually introducing these into the diet while eliminating artificial sweets has proven beneficial, improving energy levels, zest for life, and stabilizing the nervous system.

6| COLD - Cold swimming and exposure to cold conditions have gained popularity for their physical and mental health benefits. While ice-cold water is not necessary, the goal is to provide the body with water beyond the comfort limits, where one understands that life is not in danger. This practice can be done at home, transitioning from a warm shower to slightly cooler water, disrupting the state of comfort. Cooling hands, upper face, and feet with cold water yield even more effective results. This practice enhances mental resilience, courage, and the ability to navigate stressful situations by controlling the mind and internal state when adrenaline levels rise.

7| MEDITATION: There are numerous forms of meditation and practices for self-awareness, but the core essence is to understand and feel oneself and one's body. Sit in a quiet room on a chair for 15, 10, or even 5 minutes, and close your eyes. Begin without thinking or planning. Is it easy? Definitely not. Do you want to get up? Most likely, as your body seeks to escape.

What thoughts involuntarily arise in this moment of silence? If it initially feels unpleasant, and thoughts of "I am doing something wrong" overwhelm you, rest assured that you are on the right track. You are engaging in unfamiliar actions, and the body craves the old, familiar ones. However, over time, stopping and sitting in such silence will teach your body to relax, allowing your mind to guide it, not the other way around. When the mind is in control, it makes better, healthier decisions about the body daily. Even 13 minutes of meditation a day, or the ability to focus or quiet the mind, can enhance mental health, memory, and concentration. It is ideal to practice early in the morning before work, affirming that your mind will guide your body to make the best choices that day. The more frequently you practice, the easier it becomes to make improved decisions. A clearer, more focused mind leads to greater patience.

These were the main techniques that helped me enhance my mental health and overall physical condition, and I continue to practice them today. If you've lived with anxiety for an extended period, regular practice is crucial to creating lasting changes in the body. Despite occasional setbacks, these practices can help you return to your desired state faster. The key is not to let external circumstances affect you for too long – you have the power to choose how you live every minute. Learn to calm yourself, fostering respect for every person navigating life's trials, big and small.

Another aspect of my daily life is a significant reduction in coffee consumption. While coffee aids concentration, for individuals with a stressed mind (e.g., anxiety), it can provide an excessive stimulus, leading to heightened brain activity. It's advisable not to consume coffee immediately upon waking, as it interferes with the natural production of dopamine, making you feel tired quickly during the day. Reserve coffee consumption for moments when you need to concentrate on challenging tasks.

To cultivate patience, enhancing your communication skills can be particularly beneficial. For instance, focus on listening attentively, asking thoughtful questions, and avoiding "empty talk." Why advocate for speaking less? Perhaps because speaking often involves breathing through the mouth, which is considered incorrect. Moreover, indulging in "empty talk" tends to deplete your energy. If you wish to quiet your mind, consider reading serene literature before bedtime instead of engaging in aimless phone or TV usage. Writing also proves to be a valuable practice. Not only does it help articulate your thoughts, but it also facilitates the creation of new neural connections in the brain at an impressive rate. It's essential to note that this pertains to handwriting. In my experience, starting the day with writing is an excellent way to enhance focus naturally, making it easier for the mind to maintain a state of calm throughout the day. Give it a try!

AFFIRMATIONS FOR RESPECT AND PATIENCE

I am happily developing the skill of patience, taking small steps each day.

I trust that everything unfolds at the right time.

I choose not to control circumstances but to let events unfold naturally.

I respect myself and others, allowing the best outcomes to manifest without my interference.

My patience grows stronger with each passing day.

I treat myself and others with respect, avoiding the urge to rush outcomes.

I acknowledge that there is a perfect timing for everything.

Cultivating patience makes me a magnet for positive experiences.

I navigate through life's challenges because each thing has its proper time.

As I embrace self-respect, I attract individuals who respect me.

I am conscious that everything happening to me unfolds in the best possible way.

LIVE!

Sometimes in society, there's an opinion that freedom is something granted by others, that you're held captive by external forces, feeling "as if your hands were tied" due to circumstances created by someone else. If you believe this, you essentially admit that you're not in control of your life, allowing external circumstances to dictate it. Remember this fundamental rule – freedom originates in your mind. It's not physical, tangible, or visible. Freedom is a state of mind and a choice! Love, creativity, and independence are your free choices. To feel freedom, learn to express your desires and needs freely, liberate your mind from obstacles hindering self-expression, and recognize that you deserve the opportunity to express yourself. You can't expect any external source to provide skills, luck, or anything else you think you lack. Similarly, you can't expect others to take responsibility for you, be brave on your behalf, or forgive others and yourself. No one else will show you respect or see things from your perspective. Likewise, no one else will grant you freedom.

Do you travel as much as you want? Do you dance because you feel like it? Are you learning new languages or trying unusual hobbies? Do you write poetry or publish a collection of poems? Have you picked up a guitar to learn your favorite song? Have you started your own YouTube channel with kitchen tips because you love to cook? What do you want to do but haven't yet?

After developing these four great qualities, you should find the answer to how you'll create freedom for yourself. Will you still blame responsibilities, financial constraints, or your current location? Excuses will always exist. Shying away from something new is often rooted in unnecessary and contrived qualities like shyness or fear of what others might think. These are mere excuses. Doing what you love takes responsibility, courage, respect, and empathy. By developing these qualities, you'll enrich your life and cultivate a love for it.

How free you feel is determined by how much you fulfill yourself and HOW you fulfill yourself. We must constantly recharge ourselves, and we recharge by raising our vibrations. This happens when we engage in activities we truly enjoy or, more precisely, when we are inspired to direct our energy towards ourselves and the things we love. As we already know, this is one of the forms of responsibility. Is happiness synony-mous with freedom, or are they entirely unrelated concepts? Perhaps you fear that freedom will lead to loneliness?

Freedom does not equate to loneliness. If you feel lonely while thinking you are free, it might indicate a fear of being with someone due to a lack of a strong freedom of mind. If you believe that being with someone means sacrificing your freedom, be aware that true freedom lies in your mind, and the other person may not even notice, as they are preoccupied with their own freedom.

ou are free when you can assert that your words and actions align with your genuine thoughts and beliefs. To achieve freedom, you must understand what you are doing and why. Freedom is a state where, irrespective of the path's ease or difficulty, familiarity or novelty, you choose to do what you genuinely want. It involves listening to your intuition and acting in your unique style, aligning with your calling. In essence, it must reflect your identity. Living in your identity is crucial for gaining freedom. This new way of thinking and acting must become inherent in your nature. So, what is identity? Identity is YOU. It is your essence, your being. Identity is what you believe, and no one gives it to you – you create it based on your aspirations. Identity is not solely determined by your place of birth or family; they may influence your development, but a significant part of your identity lies in your thoughts, actions, and feelings. It's a choice you make every moment.

Your identity should be a self-construction. It's a creation. You are not born with an identity; it can be sought, found, and changed. Identity is not the past; it is the present. What does this mean?

If you act based on memories, you confine yourself. Memories are associated with suffering. If we had no memories, we would experience no suffering. Therefore, comprehend that the past does not exist—it's not real! Memories are mere experiences; they don't define who you are or who you can become!

First, your identity is shaped within the family, initially resembling your parents' and educators' perceptions of who you are. However, as you grow, you discern what aspects you want to develop and what truly aligns with your essence. An identity crisis emerges when you sense that your current way of life no longer resonates with you, prompting a desire for self-change. This process is normal, as only you can determine who you want to be. Identity encompasses personality—your character, unique qualities, and individuality. While personality can exist independently, identity cannot.

Living based solely on upbringing may result in an alien life, a foreign existence that may align or clash with your true identity. Recognizing this dissonance can lead to an identity crisis, a valuable opportunity for self-discovery and transformation. If you resist and persist in living within the old, mismatched identity, it may manifest as depression.

Understanding your true self allows you to live authentically. You can begin to think, act, and feel in alignment with your choices. Your identity is boundless, shaping how people perceive you worldwide. For example, the Dalai Lama is known for intelligence and balance, while Elon Musk is recognized for experimentation and entrepreneurship. Despite the diversity in people's perceptions of their personalities, their identities remain consistent and widely recognized.

Creating your identity involves discarding preconceived notions and becoming detached from societal labels. By disassociating from external identifiers like place, gender, or age, you can discern your true preferences and calling. Reflect on joyful moments, childhood passions, and consider what future you desire. Listen to yourself, understand your aspirations, and take steps to align your current actions with your desired identity.

To change your identity, decide how you want to think, feel, and act. This decision is instantaneous, though sustaining it requires forging new neural connections. Understanding the obstacles preventing this shift is essential, and this book aims to guide you through the process. Your mind and body may resist change, craving the familiar, but with self-control, you can embrace the new and recognize its superiority.

FEAR OF MISSING OUT

One of the most common fears today, FOMO (Fear of Missing Out), has largely arisen due to the development of social networks, where there is an overwhelming amount of information and events that may create the feeling of "not keeping up with something." This fear is rooted in the apprehension of rejection and being alone. It can significantly impact the individuality of young people, leading them to conform to societal norms instead of pursuing their interests and taking crucial steps in their careers. While youth pressure has always existed, the fear of missing out can currently dominate the mind. Therefore, it's essential not to succumb to everything but to be aware of your true self—stripped of addictions, money, material possessions, fear, shame, and the lessons learned through betrayals.

This journey toward freedom involves rediscovering who you really are, shedding the distractions accumulated over time, understanding your soul's depth, and letting go of learned behaviors that have obscured your identity, hindering your authenticity.

Consider your self at various stages—today, tomorrow, in a year, in 10 years, and on your 90th birthday. Reflect on commonalities and envision what memories you'd want when you're a centenarian—adventures or events.

THE MOST FREQUENT OBSTACLES TO FREEDOM OF MIND AND CREATING YOUR IDENTITY

1 | ENVY: Thinking about what others have while believing they don't deserve it automatically holds you captive. Redirect your energy from envy towards gratitude for what you have. Transform envy into inspiration by acknowledging that what fascinates or appeals to others can be achievable for you as well.

2 | NARROW THINKING: Limited thinking is a prevalent hindrance. Embrace big ideas and expand your thinking. If you can imagine it, you can achieve it. Don't let small thinking limit your joy in pursuing your goals.

3 | DISCLAIMER: Making reservations not only makes conversations boring but also dulls your life. Avoid unnecessary disclaimers—be honest about your intentions, fears, or laziness. Fabricated stories waste time and create boredom. Be truthful with yourself and others, respecting their time by avoiding fake narratives.

4 | PERMISSION - Waiting for someone else's permission to do what you want is perhaps the most significant barrier to unlocking your identity and freedom. It reflects a lack of confidence in oneself, one's thoughts, and one's abilities. Despite this, we often seek approval from our partners, parents, or other so-called "authorities" in our lives, neglecting to listen to ourselves. The mere desire to do something is a sign that it is meant for you. The first thought is usually the right one, but fear sets in, and the mind starts creating reservations, leading to a wait for permission. Seeking external permission often results in disappointment because no one else can feel your passion and subconscious belief that you will succeed. Waiting for permission mostly leads to a response based on the other person's ego. If one can be limited by another's ego, the concept of freedom becomes questionable.

5 | DISBELIEF - Faith is not solely associated with religion; it is a state of mind and body. Disbelief in your own strength is a product of your imagination. If you doubt yourself, consider revisiting the earlier parts of this book, as self-doubt is addressed among the four great qualities. It's essential to continue working with your mind.

6 | FEAR - There are numerous types of fear, some unimaginable. Fear of superiority and fear of failure can be closely related to guilt, as unconscious fears may hinder the desire for success. For instance, the fear of surpassing one's parents could stem from the concern about losing their authority and love. Fear is indeed complex. However, consider imagining yourself as the sole inhabitant of the universe, perceiving everything as part of your imagination. It might be time to release all fears and embrace doing whatever brings joy during your time on Earth.

With freedom comes responsibility, completing the circle. When you strive to act and live in alignment with your identity or live freely, you must take full responsibility for your thoughts, words, and actions. If things don't go as planned, either accept them or take steps to change them. Embrace your inner child and unleash your inner adult! Acknowledge mistakes without blame, recognizing that you acted according to your beliefs and what you thought was best at the moment, gaining insights for future changes. Making mistakes is like an intriguing game where you're unsure where or if you'll make errors at all.

In today's world, thoughts and words hold more power than ever. The more you live authentically and maintain higher vibrations, the smoother your thoughts and dreams will manifest. Understand that your task isn't to predict every step toward your goal but to allow the process, realizing that everything coming your way is a result of your desires — whether a lesson or a reward. Let everything unfold without clinging to fate or a predetermined universe plan.

When you embrace your identity, connecting with your true essence and acting on inspiration, your perspective broadens. Former concerns become insignificant, and a new gate opens, revealing a vast space that renders everything behind it small and inconsequential. Unnecessary worries dissipate, the fear of missing out vanishes, the urge to please others diminishes, and the desire to retire earlier emerges to welcome a new day, living in your newfound identity. Remember, it's all about your well-being. Avoid forcing change onto others prematurely. People around you will change when they want to, likely inspired by the positive experiences your changes bring. Refrain from expending energy on trivial matters. Learn to see the big picture, distinguishing details from small, interfering things. Focus on your growth, letting go of petty thinking. Release the need to control minutiae, and everything will work out in the best way. Enjoy the journey!

THINK BIGGER THAN THE ENVIRONMENT AROUND YOU

Epigenetics is the study of how human behavior and the environment can induce changes that affect gene function. Unlike genetic changes, epigenetic changes are reversible and do not alter the sequence of a person's DNA. However, they can modify how the body interprets the DNA sequence. What does this mean? Our genes do not inherently determine who we are! Changes in a person's consciousness can lead to physical changes in the body and behavior. We can alter our genetic destiny by activating the genes we desire and deactivating those we don't want, manipulating various environmental factors that program our genes. Some signals originate from the body, such as feelings and thoughts, while others stem from the body's response to the external environment, such as pollution or sunlight. Genes don't dictate your character or diseases; they respond to the environment! Therefore, if you're in a familiar environment and wish to change, you must learn to think differently (more expansively) than the environment around you. You can transform yourself with just one thought! Feel the change you desire before it occurs; your body will interpret it as a new environment and initiate the transformation. While this might sound easy (and complex simultaneously), we live in a remarkable era where technology allows us to explore and understand such concepts. It goes beyond the cliché of "think positive and everything will be fine" and provides evidence that "thinking positively genuinely leads to positive outcomes"! This is the essence of manifestation—your body starts to experience the desired sensations, attracting what you want to you. You don't need to figure out the "how"; maintain faith in yourself and sustain this new bodily feeling to expedite your desired outcomes. Remember that what you think about is what you attract, so think, feel, and act in alignment with the future you desire.

Science is progressing rapidly, and I am confident that epigenetics, neuroplasticity, and other relatively new fields of research will soon become mainstream, alongside healthy diet and physical activities. This is positive because, in my opinion, it will lead to a world filled with positive events.

What is happiness, health, and wealth?
These are the three most popular wishes
by people worldwide.
How you feel, how you think,
and how you act shape your identity.
What if you felt happy, thought
healthy, and acted wealthy right now?
The choice is yours,
because, as I mentioned at the beginning,
just by reading this book,
you already possess everything;
now, begin to feel and acknowledge it.

1 | CHILDHOOD - A straightforward question: What did you enjoy doing in your childhood/youth? In which moments do you recall the feeling of fulfillment? Reflect on these memories; they might conceal crucial information that will guide you back to your true self.

2 | INTUITION - Learn to develop your intuition, and, most importantly, trust it. How does it happen? To receive these peculiar "inner" thoughts or messages from the universe (call it what you want, it doesn't change the essence), all you have to do is ask! You don't always need to know the answers to all the questions instantly. But you have to ask the question and observe what happens in the next hours, days, maybe weeks. Perhaps you'll read something in a magazine that will make you ponder, or you'll receive a strange phone call or some other sign that will answer your question. Yes, it may be something entirely different from what you expected, and you might resist it at first. However, that's the essence of intuition—you receive information that your mind couldn't necessarily conceive! Therefore, try to yield to these signs and take action! Approach it with awareness, pondering, "What will this bring me?" It's highly likely that you'll experience miracles! Try to surrender to these new, unusual thoughts because for something to change, you have to embrace the unusual.

INSPIRATION. When was the last time you felt a pleasant shiver in your body, thinking of an idea, your heart seemed to flutter, or butterflies seemed to flutter in your stomach? When did something happen that sparked inspiration? As soon as something inspires you—keep your eyes and ears open because there IS something in it for you! Investigate what you see or hear, but if you feel inspiration, this delightful tingling, when your whole body lights up, then you know—there must be something. When we are genuinely inspired, our heart collaborates with our mind. This is known as the coherent state, the interaction of mind and heart. Understand that inspiration doesn't always have to be visible or tangible. Mostly it is a feeling or an emotion that arises in your body and creates a pleasant fulfillment. Find it!

FAITH. It is the awareness that as soon as you start acting in your new identity, everything you desire and what is right for you is already on its way to you. Any small step you take toward your new self is outside your normal routine, so it's a change. If you change something, the outcome changes too! Keep believing in yourself and keep doing extraordinary things because everything good is already on its way to you.

RIGHT THINKING. Remember the three ways of thinking—positive, accurate, and productive. If you can't choose one of these ways in any situation, don't dwell on it! Make an immediate change of focus, perhaps start listening to music or reading a book, but don't attempt to figure things out and create problems with wrong thinking. Bear in mind that an intensely engaged brain consumes about 40% of your energy, so use the available resources efficiently!

KNOWLEDGE. Always choose to learn something new. The more you learn, the more new neural connections form in the brain. Your experience will not change if you perceive reality with the old neural circuits. As you learn, you will change and enrich your experience! It doesn't matter whether you already know what you want your identity to be or you are still searching; learn as many new things as possible to compare and evaluate what suits you and what doesn't. Then, if you are knowledgeable about what you eat, what you wear, and why you do it, you will be much more confident in yourself. Some people enjoy teaching others about what to eat or what exercises to do. However, unless it is a doctor's or trainer's instruction, no one can know and feel better than you what you need. Gather knowledge and be firm in your convictions, so you stop being influenced by the opinions of those around you but continue to be in your new identity.

AFFIRMATIONS FOR FREEDOM AND IDENTITY

I am free to choose my own views and beliefs.

I allow myself and others to be who they are.

I honor my inner child and allow myself to be who I feel inside.

I love myself. I love myself more and more every day.

I'm proud of myself.

I believe in my abilities.

I like to be authentic.

I know what I want to be, and I'm on my way to that goal.

Even though not everyone will be happy about my new identity, the most important thing for me is to be true and open with myself.

I am grateful for my unique nature, allowing me to express myself in a way that no one else can.

I am beautiful and unique, and I am proud of how far I have come.

Every day I do the best I can, and that's a lot.

My wants and needs matter, and I gladly fulfill them without guilt.

I am aware that only I set boundaries and limits for myself.

I like to live every day the way I want.

I know how to take responsibility for myself, make brave decisions, empathize with people, respect others, and do what is my calling and what I want, and this makes me the person I am.

I'm going in the right direction.

***

Life is simple,
as long as we choose it that way.
We don't have to fight
with each other; for us,
one does not have to suffer for the other.
We just have to make a choice,
what we want to feel, think,
and how to proceed.

THE END

BEGIN!

I hope that by reading this book, you've gained insight and opened yourself up enough to realize that everything is in your hands, especially your well-being. Nevertheless, be aware that if you want everything in your life to improve from today, you need to make this choice consciously every day. Choosing to live in joy must become your new habit!

Falling back into self-pity, self-preservation is very easy and sometimes comfortable, but where will it get you? Wouldn't it be nicer to make the choice to live in joy, love, and positivity? You can get lost in the gray, gloomy, but the longer you stay there, the more boring it will become! Isn't that a good reason to start acting positively and lovingly as soon as possible? Trust me, you deserve to have the best, easiest, most beautiful, most peaceful life, and the only way you can get it is to start creating it right now and continue to create it every day. Be aware of one thing - you have the right to express your emotions if you are upset, sad, etc. But the question is how long you stay in this state. Working with yourself will help you understand how to react better in every situation - defending, attacking, or still forgiving and thinking easy thoughts that do not take away your energy and wishing the other person all the best, because you are aware that it is not related to you. This is exactly the purpose of this book - to help you cleanse yourself of everything super-fluous, old, disturbing and to let you realize that others also have to do the same homework, only they don't know it yet, and therefore you will be able to separate - what is about you and what is not.

Where do you find your strength? Can you be honest with yourself and tell yourself that now? Even if you haven't found it yet, can you honestly tell yourself that you don't yet know what it is that makes you stronger, but you would love to find it? And REALLY start looking? If you let yourself, you will find it quickly. Or you will learn what works and what doesn't, so any discovery will be valuable and lead you closer to your eternal source of power.

I hope that as you read this book and answer the questions, you don't try to please yourself by answering as "correctly" as possible. This book is really not about short-term gratification. Let it serve you as an encyclopedia, as a workbook for self-study. It sounds broad, but you don't have to memorize every word after reading it the first time - you can pick it up again and again and get inspiration for a specific practice or anything else whenever you want! Remember that it is your choice how you will spend each day. What choice did you make today? What would you change today from the moment you got up? Memorize these things and keep them in mind when you get up tomorrow! I wish that every morning of yours begins with your choice of how you want to spend your day! Be happy with your choice and appreciate every gift that comes your way.

Choose to please the self of tomorrow, the self of a month, the self of a year, and the self of 100 years. Do you want to please those very important people of yours? Then you already know what to do! I believe you will succeed! I look forward to you pursuing your calling, building your freedom, creating your unique identity! Life is really exciting, positive, multifaceted. See it! Many beautiful events are coming to you. Accept them! Build your life easily and with joy! It will be beautiful! Everything works out for you in the best possible way! Believe in yourself and love life in your new identity! Just don't sit still, because stagnation is the longest mistake anyone can make. Live!

***

BIBLIOGRAPHY

INTRODUCTION
(n.) Oxford Languages, https://languages.oup.com/google-dictionary-en/
Merzenich, D. M., Dr. et al (2013). Soft-Wired: How the New Science of Brain Plasticity Can Change Your Life (2nd ed.). Parnassus Publishing.
3. Azevedo, F. A., Carvalho, L. R., Grinberg, L. T., Farfel, J. M., Ferretti, R. E. L., Leite, R. E. P., Filho, W. J., Lent, R., & Herculano-Houzel, S. (2009). Equal numbers of neuronal and nonneuronal cells make the human brain an isometrically scaled-up primate brain. Journal of Comparative Neurology. https://doi.org/10.1002/cne.21974
4. Mattson , M. P. et al (2022). The Intermittent Fasting Revolution: The Science of Optimizing Health and Enhancing Performance. The MIT Press.
5. Arain, M., Haque, M., Johal, L., Mathur, P., & Nel, W. et al (2010). Maturation of the adolescent brain. Neuropsychiatr Dis Treat. https://doi.org/10.2147/NDT.S39776
6. SONIA, et al (2010). Cilvēks Ūdensvīra laikmetā. Hromets Poligrāfija.

WHAT YOU NEED TO KNOW ABOUT YOURSELF
1. Doidge, N. (2007). THE BRAIN THAT CHANGES ITSELF. Viking Press.
2. (n.d.). Brain Basics: The Life and Death of a Neuron. National Institute of Neurological Disorders and Stroke. https://www.ninds.nih.gov/health-information/public-education/brain-basics/brain-basics-life-and-death-neuron

3. Doidge, N. (2007). THE BRAIN THAT CHANGES ITSELF. Viking Press.

4. Sheffler, Z. M., Reddy, V., & Pillarisetty, L. S. (n.d.). et al Physiology, Neurotransmitters. National Library of Medicine. National Center for Biotechnology Information. https://www.ncbi.nlm.nih.gov/books/NBK539894/

5.Bergland, C., PhD (n.d.). How Does the Vagus Nerve Convey Gut Instincts to the Brain? Psyhology Today. https://www.psychologytoday.com/us/blog/the-athletes-way/201405/how-does-the-vagus-nerve-convey-gut-instincts-the-brain

6.Patrick, R., PhD, & Ames, B., PhD (2014, February 26). Causal link found between vitamin D, serotonin synthesis and autism in new study. ScienceDaily. https://www.sciencedaily.com/releases/2014/02/140226110836.htm

THE FIRST STEP

1.(1999). Psiholoģijas vārdnīca. Mācību grāmata.

2.(n.d.). Adolescent Brain Development. Kids Health. https://www.kidshealth.org.nz/adolescent-brain-development

3.Kudrjavcevs, I. (2014). Dzīvības spēks. Kā saudzēt, stiprināt un vairot dzīvības enerģiju sevī. Apgāds Zvaigzne ABC.

4.Dispenza, J., Dr. (2017). BECOMING SUPERNATURAL. How Common People Are Doing the Uncommon. Hay House, Inc.

5.Duhigg, C. (2012). THE POWER OF HABIT: Why We Do What We Do in Life and Business. Random House.

6.Andrew Huberman. (2022, December 5). Using Caffeine to Optimize Mental & Physical Performance | Huberman Lab Podcast 101 [Video]. YouTube. https://www.youtube.com/watch?v=iw97uvIge7c

7.Fekseuss, H. (2011). DARI, KO ES VĒLOS! Grāmata par ietekmēšanu. Apgāds Zvaigzne ABC.

8.Parvez, H. et al (2022, October 11). Fear of responsibility and its causes. PsychMechanics. https://www.psychmechanics.com/fear-of-responsibility/

9.Andrew Huberman. (2021, April 12). The Science of How to Optimize Testosterone & Estrogen | Huberman Lab Podcast #15 [Video]. YouTube. https://www.youtube.com/watch?v=qJX-Khu5UZwk

THE THIRD STEP

1. Behary , W. T. et al (2008). Disarming the Narcissist: Surviving and Thriving with the Self-Absorbed. New Harbinger Publications.

2., 3. (1999). Psiholoģijas vārdnīca. Mācību grāmata.

4. Sanda , I. (2016). Mīli sevi! Apgāds Zvaigzne ABC.

5. Northrup , C., M.D. (2018). Dodging Energy Vampires: An Empath's Guide to Evading Relationships That Drain You and Restoring Your Health and Power. Hay House, Inc.

6. Ettensohn , M., PsyD. et al (2016). Unmasking Narcissism: A Guide to Understanding the Narcissist in Your Life. Althea Press.

7. Dyer , J. (2020). Empaths and Narcissists: 2 Books in 1. Pristine Publishing.

8. Carter , S., & Sokol, J. (2005). Help! I'm in Love with a Narcissist. M. Evans & Company.

THE FOURTH STEP

1.(n.d.). Patience. Cambridge Dictionary. https://dictionary.cambridge.org/dictionary/english/patience

2.Lu Parker. (2018, March 12). Jay Shetty Talks the Importance of Your Breath [Video]. YouTube. https://www.youtube.com/watch?v=9oMt7TDJR4E

3.Penguin Books UK. (2022, February 7). 5 Ways To Improve Your Breathing with James Nestor [Video]. YouTube. https://www.youtube.com/watch?v=f6yAY1oZUOA

4.Marksberry, K. et al (2012, August 10). Take a Deep Breath. The American Institute of Stress. https://www.stress.org/take-a-deep-breath

5.Penguin Books UK. (2022, February 7). 5 Ways To Improve Your Breathing with James Nestor [Video]. YouTube. https://www.youtube.com/watch?v=f6yAY1oZUOA

6.Herring, M. P., O'Connor, P. J., & Dishman, R. K. (2010, February 22). The effect of exercise training on anxiety symptoms among patients: A systematic review. National Library of Medicine. https://pubmed.ncbi.nlm.nih.gov/20177034/

7.Clifton, T., et al CPT (2021, October 22). Hit the Reset Button: Running for Anxiety. Healthline. https://www.healthline.com/health/fitness/running-for-anxiety

8.Harvard Medical School (2008, May 1). The dubious practice of detox. Harvard Health Publishing. https://www.health.harvard.edu/staying-healthy/the-dubious-practice-of-detox

9.Calbom, C. et al (2005). The Wrinkle Cleanse (3rd ed.). Avery.

10.Andrew Huberman. (2022, April 4). Using Deliberate Cold Exposure for Health and Performance | Huberman Lab Podcast #66 [Video]. YouTube. https://www.youtube.com/watch?v=pq6WHJzOkno

11.Andrew Huberman. (2022, October 31). How Meditation Works & Science-Based Effective Meditations | Huberman Lab Podcast #96 [Video]. YouTube. https://www.youtube.com/watch?v=wTBSGgbIvsY&t=7103s

FREEDOM

1.Gupta, M., & Sharma, A. (2021, July 6). Fear of missing out: A brief overview of origin, theoretical underpinnings and relationship with mental health. National Library of Medicine. https://www.ncbi.nlm.nih.gov/pmc/articles/PMC8283615/

2.Dispenza , J. (2014). You Are the Placebo: Making Your Mind Matter. Hay House.

3.,4. Dispenza, J., Dr. (2017). BECOMING SUPERNATURAL. How Common People Are Doing the Uncommon. Hay House, Inc.

get your life back on track
NOW

IEVA ELZA ZAHAROVA

2023